Books by John David Morley

PICTURES FROM THE WATER TRADE

IN THE LABYRINTH

In the Labyrinth

In the Labyrinth

by JOHN DAVID MORLEY

The Atlantic Monthly Press
BOSTON / NEW YORK

FIRST EDITION

LIBRARY OF CONGRESS CATALOGING-IN-PUBLICATION DATA

Morley, John David, 1948–
  In the labyrinth.

  1. World War, 1939–45—Fiction. 2. Czechoslovakia—
History—1938–1945—Fiction. 3. Czechoslovakia—History
—1945–   —Fiction. I. Title.
PS3563.08718815 1986   813'.54   86-3409
ISBN 0-87113-070-X

BP

Published simultaneously in Canada

PRINTED IN THE UNITED STATES OF AMERICA

To my parents

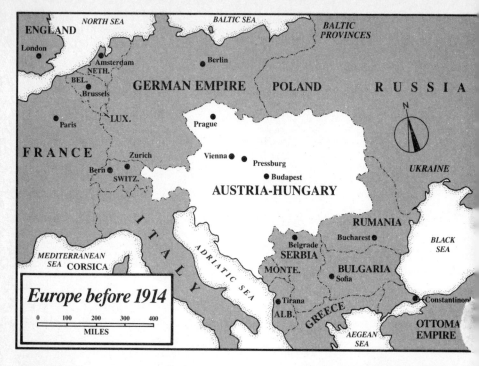

Europe, 1939–1945

MILES
0 100 200 300 400

Europe after 1945

MILES
0 100 200 300 400

Author's Note

In the Labyrinth tells a true story; that is to say, it is based for the most part on taped conversations with the man who appears in the following pages under the name of Joseph Pallehner. It also incorporates material from interviews I have had with a contemporary of Pallehner's who was a fellow inmate at Leopoldov Prison, from the published memoirs of another prisoner, and from a variety of historical works. Historically identifiable names and dates have been verified wherever possible. The substance is fact, not fiction. As the first-person narrator of Pallehner's experiences, however, I have inevitably filtered them through my own imagination. I have had to make my own selections, to paraphrase, to amplify, to supply my own interpretations and, occasionally, my own inventions, so long as to do so has not meant to impinge on historical veracity.

Contents

In the Labyrinth

Arrest

I HADN'T quite finished my breakfast when the doorbell rang. My wife had just poured me a fresh cup of coffee, half a slice of bread and honey lay uneaten on the plate in front of me. That didn't seem to matter at the time. I pushed back my chair, went out into the hall and opened the front door. A young man in uniform standing outside asked me if my name was Joseph Pallehner. I said it was. The young man told me I was under arrest.

I asked him why, but he didn't know. Behind his shoulder I saw blue sky and bright reflections from the snow and I asked him instead, thinking of the inconvenience this would cause my arrangements for the day, by whose authority I was arrested.

"In the name of the occupation army," he replied, and showed me the warrant for my arrest.

"I suppose it'll just be a formality. Do you want me to go with you now?"

He hesitated. "I can let you have an hour."

"An hour? What for? I don't need an hour. We might as well go now."

He shrugged his shoulders and took out a cigarette. I left him standing outside and went to tell my wife.

A quarter of an hour later we left the house. Against my

wishes I was carrying a bag with a few necessaries that my wife had persuaded me to take. I resented my wife's insisting on my taking the bag. I told her I didn't need it, for I would soon be coming home; there had been a mistake. But my wife said nothing and packed the bag.

From the suburb where I lived we caught a train into the city. We were going to police headquarters, the young man said, but he knew no more than that himself. That was all the information he had been given. Perhaps I had good reasons to expect my immediate release, he said, but that was none of his affair. He chatted amiably and offered me cigarettes. I wondered if the young man offered me cigarettes because I was his prisoner, but I accepted them in any case and put two in my coat pocket.

At the entrance to police headquarters the young man produced a set of papers, which were stamped and countersigned. Another guard led me through an inner courtyard to a building at the back. We went up several flights of stairs until we had reached the third or fourth floor. There was a great deal of coming and going on the stairs and in the corridors; officials, for the most part in uniform, carrying bundles of files. On benches that stretched all the way down the corridor sat a long line of silent men: the subject, it occurred to me, of all these files the officials were carrying, indeed, of the activities throughout the entire building. At the end of the corridor I was turned over to another guard; papers were again exchanged and countersigned. A door was opened and I stepped into an enormous room.

There must have been a couple of hundred men inside. A gallery ran around the entire room, deep shelves were bracketed to the walls; perhaps it had been used as an archive or a library. But instead of books or files the shelves were now packed with men, sitting or lying, quite comfortably it seemed, three or four shelves high. A hollow

4

murmuring hung on the walls, like tapestries of sound, bringing an image to my mind of a cathedral studded with pigeons. Every few minutes the door through which I had entered was opened, and a name or names would be called out, new arrivals came in; thus there was a constant clambering up and down as the shelves were vacated or occupied. I soon understood the reason for these curious seating arrangements. The floor was bare concrete and the building unheated: it was warmer on the wooden shelves.

I found myself a niche and soon fell into conversation with a group of men. Some of them, like myself, had only arrived that morning, but others had been there since the previous day. There were men of a great variety of nationalities and from all walks of life — German, Czech, Russian, Hungarian, stateless persons, politicians, generals, administrators, currency smugglers and black marketeers, all in the temporary custody of the American occupation army and awaiting summary judgment on charges known or unknown in an ad hoc military court that convened in a small room farther down the corridor. Most of these men knew the charges that had been brought against them, but there were others, like myself, who had no idea why they had been arrested.

I had been in this room for several hours when my name was called out. I was led down the corridor into a much smaller room that I took to be the court. About half a dozen men stood at the back of the room, facing a table on a dais at which a smooth-faced, middle-aged man, apparently the judge, was conducting the hearings. He was aided by a clerk, who sat at another desk behind two stacks of files: one for the cases that had already been heard, another for those that were still to come. The clerk took the files he handed to the judge from one stack and replaced those he was handed back on the other.

I stood in the line of men and awaited my turn. I was amazed at the speed with which judgment was passed. A few brief exchanges with the accused, lasting perhaps three or four minutes, and then the sentence: acquitted! six months! eighteen months! The judge snapped one file shut and was already leafing through the next.

"What is your name?"

"Joseph Pallehner."

"Nationality?"

"German."

I could not see what was in my file, but from where I was standing I saw that it was a very slim file, not more than two or three pages at most. The judge frowned and turned over a page.

"Were you a member of the party?"

"No."

"What are you here for?"

"I have no idea."

The judge leafed one page back, brooded, leafed forward, "Perhaps there has been a mistake . . ."

I waited anxiously while the judge pondered my file.

"So far as I am concerned there is no case against you. But I see that you are a former citizen of Czechoslovakia. Perhaps they are interested in you. So —"

The judge laid my file on the table beside him and reached for the next. Without knowing what verdict had been reached I found myself escorted outside and back to the room where I had originally been taken.

In the evening, when the hearings for that day had come to an end, there were still some forty or fifty men left in the room whose cases had not yet been decided. We were given bread, a bowl of soup, and blankets. I lay down on a shelf and was grateful for my coat. In the niche above me a haggard man in tattered clothes who said he had fought at Stalingrad complained bitterly of the hardships of the war and the injustice of his fate — interned first by the Russians, now by the Americans, when would it end? Uneasily I asked myself the same question. But what could they do to me? What had I done? Nothing. Satisfied that my conscience was clear, I soon fell asleep.

They came for me early the next morning. I expected there would be a second hearing, perhaps a few further formalities, and then I would be free to go home. But to my surprise the guard escorted me down the corridor — as full of waiting men as on the day before, as if nothing had changed, nobody moved on — back to a barred gateway on the other side of the police headquarters. Still inside the courtyard the guard stopped and took a pair of handcuffs out of his pocket.

I asked him where I was being taken.

"To Dachau."

"To Dachau!" I echoed in astonishment. "What on earth for?"

"For further questioning. I can tell you no more than that myself. My orders are to take you there, *basta*."

I objected to the handcuffs.

"I've no intention of trying to escape. You have my word."

"Your word!"

The guard laughed and snapped the handcuff over my wrist.

Because of blockages farther down the line the journey to Dachau took much longer than usual. I felt less at ease on this journey than I had on the day before. The guard stared morosely out of the window, offered no cigarettes. It crossed my mind that the marked difference between yesterday's escort and today's might be understood to imply a deterioration in the prospects of my case — I dismissed this thought as foolish, but it was worrying that such thoughts should be occurring to me at all.

In the vast bleak camp the huts seemed to huddle under the wind that came scudding across the open plain. The weather was clear but very cold.

At the entrance to the camp I was turned over to American soldiers. My bag was checked in, the contents listed, the list countersigned and removed with the bag. In the guardroom I stripped to the waist and raised my arms as instructed. They were looking for an SS blood-group identification tattooed into the armpit; but of course I had never had anything to do with the SS.

When my clothes had been searched I was allowed to get dressed again. I was led off to a second barrack, a quarter of an hour's walk from the entrance. The size of the camp astonished me.

The second barrack was divided down the middle, cells on either side. There were apertures in the cell doors large enough for a man to put his head through. The guard who had escorted me unlocked a cell at the end of the barrack and motioned me in, saying in a not unfriendly voice, "A hearing of your case will be arranged at the earliest possible date. So long as you are in this camp you will remain in solitary confinement, but don't worry, you will be treated well."

With that he locked the door and for the first time in almost forty-eight hours I found myself alone.

I had never been in a cell. I looked around with curiosity. The cell seemed to be quite large and was even reasonably furnished, with a bed, a chair and a table. Above all it was heated. I took off my fur coat and laid it on the bed. I had been allowed to keep my own clothes, which I took to mean that I was not expected to stay very long in the camp. I was still perfectly confident that the mistake that had been made in ordering my arrest would soon be cleared up and that I would be allowed to go home. Cheered by this thought, and gradually succumbing to the pleasant warmth in the barrack, I at last dozed off.

But the days passed and nothing happened. I was fed well, allowed regular exercise, could receive and write letters. I had two letters from my wife. She had been to see an influential friend of ours, who had interceded with high American officials on my behalf and assured her that steps would immediately be taken to clear up the unfortunate misunderstanding that had led to my arrest. The children were well, she was confident of the outcome of the case, I should not lose heart. I was cheered by this letter and reread it several times a day.

One morning, a week after my arrival, I was escorted to a part of the camp that did not belong to the American zone. In a compound formed by the surrounding barracks I waited for some minutes while my escort conferred in English with a small man in spectacles and civilian clothes. We happened to be standing by a flagpole. I glanced up idly and with a shock recognized the flag: I was in the Czechoslovakian zone.

Before I had time to consider the implications of this new situation I was asked to follow the man in civilian clothes into one of the barracks. I entered a large room bare of anything but a table and two chairs at one end. Behind this table sat a man wearing the uniform of a British major. He got up with a smile and greeted me in German, but from the few words he exchanged with the civilian who took a seat beside him at the table, I gathered that the British major was in fact Czech.

The major was courteous and apologetic.

"I have been asked by my American colleagues to review

your case. First of all I owe you an apology for the inconvenience you must have been caused. The administrative chaos, you realize . . . it will take years before we get it all sorted out. And in the meantime mistakes do of course happen. Most unfortunate, but, well . . . there we are."

He spread his hands and smiled again. The civilian beside him, arms folded and eyes fixed on the floor, did not smile.

The major took a file out of the table drawer and handed it to the civilian. So far as I could tell it was the same file I had seen in the hands of the judge at the police headquarters a week before.

"The Americans have asked me," the major continued, "if the Czechoslovakian government is interested in your extradition. Apparently such a request has been filed. I must say I am rather puzzled. Nothing in your record seems to me to warrant such a request. You spent the war in Pressburg — or in Bratislava, as I should more correctly say — conducting your business. This business was only marginally relevant to German activities there or to the interests of the fascist Slovakian government. It may be held against you that you were a member of the German Party in Slovakia, but that alone hardly constitutes a charge and does not justify your extradition. So, I do not see how it can be considered that there is any case against you at all. Perhaps you can shed some light on the matter. . . ."

I said that I was quite as mystified as the major. I could contribute no information that might help to explain the matter.

The major turned to the civilian, who shook his head and placed the file on the table.

"Anyway," said the major, "so far as I'm concerned Czechoslovakia has no interest in requesting your extradition."

He got up and held out his hand.

"Good-bye."

"Then what happens now?" I asked, as we shook hands.

"That is no longer my responsibility. That will be for the Americans to decide."

The Americans would decide. Then everything was clear. There was now nothing for them to do but to release me.

And two days later they did come to fetch me. I was led back to the Czechoslovakian zone, to a patch of land between the barracks and the outer fence. A truck stood ready, the gate was open, the road led out to a free world beyond. A man walked away from the truck, escorted by two guards. The guards halted, the man walked on, alone, toward me, I toward him; for a moment his face seemed familiar, but already he had passed and, hesitating for a moment, I was told by the guards to climb into the truck: so climbed, took a seat inside beside an American soldier and just caught the words "there's your fifteenth man then" before the engines roared and the truck rolled out, not west but east, as became clear to me when it was already too late, when no amount of explanation, no pleas, no denials, nothing could any longer help, for within two hours, on March the fourteenth, 1947, we had already crossed the Czechoslovakian border.

The American escort that had accompanied the truck turned back at the border. The border guards were prompt. There were brief transactions with documents, a counting of heads inside the truck, and the vehicle was waved on. I sat by a Czech guard now at the open end of the truck, and with a sense of dreadful familiarity watched the white landscape fly past.

There was an incident at a small town not far from the border. I knew the town — a woman friend of mine whom I had often visited before the war had lived there for many years. Maybe she still did, I did not know, but I was no longer welcome now. When the convoy called a halt and the prisoners were allowed to stretch their legs in the marketplace, word got around among the local people and we soon found ourselves surrounded by an angry crowd brandishing pitchforks and cudgels — only the intervention of our armed escort prevented outright murder. We were quickly herded back into the truck and drove on until nightfall, when the convoy drove through the prison gates in Pilsen.

Conditions here were much tougher than they had been in Dachau. On arrival we surrendered our clothes and all personal belongings — rings, wristwatches and even spectacles. The Czech warder who handed out our prison clothes told us that Konrad Henlein, the former leader of the National Socialists in the Sudetenland, had committed suicide in a cell here in Pilsen by slashing his wrists with a fragment of his glasses. Since then prevention of suicide had become a major concern. The fifteen of us were kept in solitary confinement in the same wing. We were under constant observation. The lights remained on in the cells day and night, and we had orders to lie only on our back, facing the control window in the door.

I measured out my cell in paces — five and a half paces from window to door. There was a low iron bedstead with a straw pallet and a blanket, a cup, a bowl, and a hole in the floor with a bucket in which to defecate.

I came to know this cell in Pilsen in every detail. The hours became days, the days became weeks, with never the slightest change. I was awoken each morning at six, cleaned and rinsed my bucket, swabbed the floor with a rag, folded my blanket and smoothed the pallet for inspection at seven, when I was ordered out into the corridor to report to the guard. Coffee and bread shortly after seven, then the resumption of my solitary silence, interrupted at noon and six by the appearance of meager, indigestible meals.

These were not the only signs that the world continued to exist outside. Sometimes in the night I heard terrible, agonized cries, cries that seemed to come up through stone floors from far below with undiminished clarity. Apparently men were being tortured here, and more: great trouble was taken to prevent suicide only in order to save prisoners for hanging. My evidence for this was a terse valediction scratched at the foot of the door of my cell: trial on the 5th began at 16.00, ended at 17.00, execution tomorrow. This sentence, the screams I heard at night, engraved themselves on my imagination, in solitude already nervous for want of tangible experience, until gradually I began to live in fear of my own torture, my own hanging, as though this had now become so natural an aspect of my surroundings that it no longer required any particular reason.

Apart from the hands and the lower half of a face that I saw twice daily when my meals were passed in to me through the hatch in my door, my only contact with other human beings was during the few minutes I stood in the corridor each morning. Although it was forbidden to talk with other prisoners, I soon learned the art of projecting whispers that made communication with my cell neighbors possible, even at the risk of having my rations halved.

My cell neighbor to the right was a man in middle age, like myself, by the name of Oberle, whom I had once met in Pressburg. Oberle had been the managing director of a German-owned timber company that operated in Slovakia, among other things supplying materials for the construction of army barracks there. Just before the final collapse of the

Reich he had evacuated all the machinery from the company's sawmills in Slovakia and put them in storage in Germany — he refused to say where, so the Czechs had demanded his extradition. I learned this information in the course of a week's furtive conversations in the corridor each morning.

My other neighbor was a young man in his mid-twenties, pale and already very thin. His name was Sellner and he came from Kremnitz, a town in central Slovakia close to the Tatra Mountains, where his father had been mayor. Sellner was already so pale and thin because, regardless of the merits of his case, he knew he was a definite candidate for hanging: he had been a member of the Waffen SS. Through the chance juxtaposition of our cells in Pilsen I soon came to play a vital part in Sellner's life.

I and the fourteen other men who had been together on the transport from Dachau spent forty-seven days in our initial solitary confinement in Pilsen. We had an exact record of the passage of time because on April 18 we were unexpectedly summoned into the corridor and informed that in the early hours of that morning Dr. Josef Tiso, former president of the Slovak republic, had been executed. "This is how collaborators with the enemies of the Czechoslovakian people will be punished," we were admonished. The news of Tiso's death caused a considerable shock. It was an omen of what was to come.

About two weeks after this announcement we were once again suddenly called out of our cells, marched down the corridor and out into the yard. The personal belongings that had been confiscated on our arrival were restored. In pairs the men were handcuffed and climbed into a waiting truck. I found myself paired with my cell neighbor Sellner.

The truck brought us to the station. We boarded the last car of a train waiting in a separate siding. Not a word was said as to our destination, but the train was soon traveling south — not to Prague, then, but perhaps to Brünn and Pressburg.

The train reached Brünn without incident. Here there was a halt for an hour before the train resumed its journey, again traveling in a southeast direction — clearly the destination would be Pressburg. I sat by the window and looked out at a landscape over which the war seemed to have passed without leaving any trace.

The fifteen men had been allotted three compartments in the last car. We were allowed to talk, but conversation was desultory, each man preoccupied with his own thoughts. In each compartment sat a guard, usually dozing, with a machine gun resting on his knees. From time to time a couple of men would get up to go to the toilet, which was at the rear end of the car. I had diarrhea and was obliged to go several times; an awkward and unpleasant situation, for the man to whom I was handcuffed somehow had to squeeze in and crouch down beside me. But Sellner was patient and uncomplaining.

Not long after we had left Brünn I began to have the feeling that my right arm was growing damp. I turned to Sellner, who was sitting beside me with his eyes shut, and saw that he was dripping with sweat; so much so, that his sweat had soaked through my own shirtsleeve.

"Aren't you feeling well?"

Sellner shook his head.

"I think I'd better — we —"

We got up and made our way back to the toilet. But Sellner did not go to the toilet. "It's air I need," he said, opening the door onto the observation platform and stepping out. I stood behind him, my shoulder holding the door open, one foot on the platform grid, one foot still in the corridor. Through the grid I saw the ground rush away beneath us, two shining tracks, the sleepers between like a ripple of shadows, fast and dark and dangerous; and perhaps this was why I braced myself, sensing what was about to happen, just before Sellner jerked me forward as he tried to pitch himself over the rail. With the same movement with which Sellner brought his head down I jammed my leg against the rail and pulled him back up. Sellner tore his arm away and yelled "Jump, you fool! Jump!" and I began to fight for my life — my life his life, for we were chained together. The tracks hurtled away from us, for several minutes Sellner grappled with me desperately between the door and the rail, first cursing me and then begging me to let go. But I was the stronger and the heavier man, thank God. With my free hand I slapped Sellner across the face to bring him to his senses and pulled him back inside. The two of us leaned panting against the door, enemies tied to each other, and I said angrily "Why the hell should I kill myself for you?" but Sellner did not answer until, when he got his breath back and we were squatting on the rumbling floor of the train, he told me the full story.

At the time Sellner got on the train at Pilsen he knew it was taking him to his death. As soon as he arrived at the prison he had been told that he was being sent to Slovakia in order to be hanged. That was why they had taken away his belt and his shoelaces — to prevent him from hanging himself. A prisoner already condemned to death, they said, was not allowed anything in his cell that he might conceivably use to take his own life. That was his captors' privilege. He would stand trial, but there was no hope: he was a condemned man. Every day a warder looked into his cell and cursed him.

"It won't be long now. In Slovakia you will be hanged."

During the weeks of his solitary confinement he had gradually given up all hope. That was why he had tried to jump, tried to kill himself, would have killed himself had I not held him back.

Sellner would rather have died now in Moravia than later in Slovakia. He did not want to go home to be hanged. He was the son of a long-established German family in an old German settlement, thought and felt as a German, although outside the house he had been brought up speaking Slovak and had worn a Slovakian uniform when he was drafted into an artillery regiment in the autumn of 1939. Only the emblem with a swastika, sewn onto his uniform, symbolized his attachment to the local German battalion and to the German cause in general.

As a bilingual German-Slovak speaker he was detailed to a propaganda unit that in 1941 was sent to Russia, where he worked as a translator and broadcaster. During the retreat in 1944 he was holed up in Odessa, escaped to Rumania, Hungary and finally back to Slovakia just as the August uprising began. The Slovakian army was in disarray and Sellner joined the local unit of the home guard when fighting began between Germans and Slovak partisans. Two weeks later he was captured, was put to work behind partisan lines on the construction of a secret airstrip, and under the German threat of reprisals for all prisoners not returned alive was released soon after. But in the bitter fighting of the uprising the massacre of local civilian populations had already taken place both on the German and the Slovak sides.

In January 1945 Sellner was forcibly recruited into the Waffen SS. Toward the end of the war the conscription of all so-called *Volksdeutsche* — ethnic Germans who were not citizens of the Reich — meant service in the Waffen SS. Enlistment in other units was, if not impossible, at least very difficult, which for those who were captured or returned, like Sellner, after the war meant death as criminals and traitors. But Sellner did not see himself as either a criminal or a traitor — on the contrary, he had remained true to the cause of German arms. And during the critical weeks of the uprising, with which the charges later brought against him were concerned, he had in any case been a prisoner of the partisans, whose women had tied weights to his testicles and horsewhipped him for good measure.

Sellner became one of the so-called werewolves, fighting on in the forests of Bohemia until May 1945, when he was captured by the Americans on the Bavarian border. He drifted through various camps, escaped, took cover in the Bavarian Forest, got a job, became engaged and lived unmolested in Passau for about a year. He was again arrested and after weeks in half a dozen camps or prisons arrived in Dachau at about the same time as myself.

There were no interrogations in Dachau, and not until he reached Pilsen did he learn the reason for his extradition: that he had been in the Waffen SS and would accordingly be sentenced to death. But the precise charges — for the fact of membership in an organization need not by itself constitute an indictment — were not made known to him until he reached Pressburg.

Shortly before this point (for we were still squatting in the corridor of a train somewhere between Brünn and Pressburg) Sellner's story came to an end, but when we met again in the fortress of Leopoldov some years later he told me the grim sequel.

In the cells of the central police administration in Pressburg Sellner was beaten and tortured until he was half dead. Had a confession been required he would have confessed, but at first his tormentors wanted something of him that he could not give: an identification. He was shown photographs of corpses and asked to identify them. They were the corpses of partisans, Communists and gypsies who had been shot in Kremnitz during the Slovak uprising in August 1944. The bodies had been exhumed and photographed in the spring of the following year — almost six months after they had been interred. In this advanced state of decomposition naturally not much more than the outlines of the bodies were recognizable, but Sellner's interrogators assumed that he would nonetheless be in a position to say, since — this was a fact, was it not — he had been in charge of the firing squad. This accusation had not been brought by an eyewitness of the scene, but by someone who claimed to have spoken with an eyewitness. Sellner was never confronted with this witness, not even at his trial. The testimony was accepted in the form of written evidence.

When it became clear that Sellner would never be able to supply any information about the corpses, he was asked to sign a confession admitting responsibility for the deaths. But Sellner was now in such constant pain during his intermittent bouts of consciousness that it mattered little whether he was beaten more or not; earlier, perhaps, he might have signed, but now he refused. Twice he tried to escape from his pain, once by attacking a warder, in the hope that he would subsequently be beaten to death, once by running head down into a stone wall. He learned how hard it was to die.

After two or three weeks he was removed from his cell in Pressburg. He could not walk. They dragged him by his feet through the corridors and tossed him like a sack onto a truck in the prison yard. His jaw, more or less repaired after he had been blown up in Russia, was again broken. The only purpose of this last journey, he learned, was to execute him in Banska Bystrica, which as the origin of the Slovak uprising so brutally beaten down by the German invaders should have the right to carry out its own vengeance.

Sellner had already been sentenced to death in his absence by the court in Banska Bystrica, so he arrived with nothing to expect but his execution. He was put in a wing reserved for condemned men. Every second cell on the corridor remained empty, it seemed as a precaution against contact between the prisoners. For the same reason no exercise was allowed. The isolation of each man in his cell was complete.

He waited for death. A week after his arrival the first execution was carried out; a Slovak collaborator, he learned afterwards. The condemned man was fetched at dawn. Sellner heard footsteps, keys, a door swung open, murmurs of voices, footsteps, silence. The same procedure a few days later, then for weeks, months, nothing, no footsteps, keys, voices. But the third time it happened differently. They came in the night. The victim was two cells down, a Czech; Sellner had heard him speak. And perhaps because they came upon him unawares he resisted, but not uttering a sound, strangely, offering resistance only with his feet and arms: the sounds of friction on walls and floors, thuds, the final silence. From then on Sellner's composure, those patterns, made possible by forewarning, that had settled icily in his mind like frost, was easily disturbed. Unexplained footsteps, warders rattling keys, or the sound of a sprung lock at unhabitual times and Sellner leaped to his feet: here they were, the time had come at last! At such moments his heart seemed to stop beating for minutes at a stretch.

Such moments apart, he learned that one could become accustomed to all things, even to this daily expectation of dying. Habit took the sting out of the fear of death. If they hanged him, it was over, if not, what worse could they do? It was a simple reckoning. He drew a line, forgot the present, recalled the past, a memory on which his thoughts could turn. With the connivance of memory and imagination he escaped his present fears. It did not surprise him that he seldom heard resistance when the time had come. He knew that he himself would offer none. There would be no voice in his throat: no speech: blank shock, a drained mind. He would go without a sound.

Passive but prepared, already well accustomed to the necessity of death while still entrenched in life, Sellner awaited this moment for over two hundred days. During this time six executions were carried out.

Meanwhile friends and relatives outside had succeeded in having his case brought up for review. A retrial was ordered. Under the procedures of the People's Courts at that time the defendant was required to prove his innocence, not the prosecution his guilt. Sellner was confident. As a volunteer in the home guard he had for a while done sentry duty in Kremnitz Prison, where, at the request of his father, impotent in the face of arbitrary punishment and the suspension of formal justice, he had been in a position to help a number of people whose lives had been endangered. These people appeared in court to speak on his behalf. The court, however, argued that precisely the fact of his having been in a position to help people burdened him with the moral responsibility for the fate of those many more whom he had not been able to help, and on this and a number of other counts passed a sentence of life imprisonment.

Who could say what Sellner had done or not done? Ever since the murder of the German officers who were members of Colonel Ott's diplomatic mission, with which the Slovak uprising had begun, there had been confusion and butchery, reprisals and counterreprisals in bloody succession. The trial was a transaction of a kind, a price had been demanded and a payment made, and the accumulation of a guilt that had long remained unclaimed was given a name in which, at least in part, it could finally be expiated.

Journey into the Past

I ARRIVED in Bratislava on my forty-fifth birthday. The town in which I was born in 1902 had at that time been known by other names: in Hungarian Pozsony, in German Pressburg. It was not until after the First World War, when the state of Czechoslovakia came into being, that the town also acquired the name Bratislava. I used all three names, according to which language I spoke. Until I went to school I spoke almost no Hungarian, but thereafter, for many years, I was allowed to speak no other language at home, with the result that I entered adult life speaking several languages fluently but none perfectly.

I owed allegiance to as many states as I did languages. For the first sixteen years of my life I was a Hungarian citizen, the loyal subject of a Hungarian monarch. Hungarian was chic. This was the preferred language at the rowing club and in the affluent German drawing rooms, where the only Slovaks in attendance were those serving on the house staff. Slovaks were for the most part servants and their language was accordingly the language of servants. I and my classmates were every bit as conservative as our elders in rejecting the enforced transfer of our loyalty as citizens from the stylish Hungarian monarchy to a creation called the Republic of Czechoslovakia, in which the servers claimed equality with those whom they had hitherto served. Thus the struggles between rich and poor, which everywhere in Europe became struggles of class, were overlaid in the eastern countries of central Europe by the rivalry of ethnic factions.

In the Hungarian-speaking school I attended there was a boycott of Slovak; entire classes failed their new language exams. On the Slovak side, with the same obstinacy, an official language of instruction began to be used in the schools that for many of the pupils was unintelligible. Gradually, however, the Czechs in Bohemia and Moravia and the Slovaks in Slovakia found acceptance for their languages. When I completed my business studies in Vienna in 1922 I was apprenticed to a wholesaler in Prague partly in order to learn Czech; and on my return to the city now officially known as Bratislava I found a knowledge of Slovak indispensable.

In the offices of the ironmongery that my great-great-grandfather had founded at the end of the eighteenth century I learned the business from the bottom up. When my father retired seven years later I took over the firm. At the age of twenty-eight I found myself in an influential position in the Slovakian business community, at the top of a multinational pyramid made up of two and a half million Slovaks, more than half a million Hungarians, a hundred and fifty thousand Germans, eighty thousand Jews, and a sprinkling of Poles and Ukrainians.

I was busy during the 1930s. I expanded the wholesale business, added retail outlets and took over a tileworks in Deutsch-Proben. I resisted pressure for Slovak participation in my business and maintained good relations with my Jewish competitors. As a freemason I continued to cultivate in adult life the exclusive Hungarian conspiracy that had begun during my schooldays. Freemasonry was soon challenged by another love: the Slovak-Russian girl from Odessa whom I courted for two years in Vienna before she accompanied me back to Pressburg as my wife.

Among the many national interests of which I was bound to take cognizance one article of faith went unquestioned: my first loyalty was to the ethnic German community, not to the state of which I had nominally become a citizen. Under the old Hungarian monarchy there had been a less rigid distinction; Hungarian Germans were also Hungarian patriots, but Czech Germans did not turn into Czech patriots. For those Germans living in Slovakia, as opposed to Bohemia and Moravia, relationships with the state of which they had become subjects were further vitiated by Slovak antagonism to the supremacy of Prague and the virtual dictatorship of Czech interests. This was not what the Slovaks had been promised in the Treaty of Pittsburgh, this was not the common state of Czechs and Slovaks in which Slovakian autonomy was to be respected. Thus the interests of Slovak separatists and German nationalists came to coincide.

From the tranquility of my Pressburg villa I followed Hitler's rise to power and the tumultuous passage of Konrad Henlein through the Sudetenland. I had no objections to the prospect of closer relations between Czechoslovakia and the Reich; my business would obviously benefit. But these events still seemed remote and I was not sufficiently alert, perhaps not sufficiently involved, to pay much attention to the occasional more thoughtful opinion I heard. My friend Esterhazy, for example, criticized the Sudeten German Party for establishing a precedent that would crack the foundation of any multinational state; here was a party whose followers were recruited solely on an ethnic principle, to which nobody had access except by the accident of his birth. What would happen if Czechs, Slovaks, Hungarians and Jews all formed parties of this kind? Where would the common interest, the true spirit of democracy lie? But I was not persuaded by arguments of this kind. I was young, prosperous, my wife had just borne me a son. I believed in peaceful coexistence. My own wife was of mixed Slovak and Russian ancestry. Wasn't Henlein's mother herself a Czech? And Franz Karmasin, Henlein's deputy in Slovakia, who happened to be present that evening in my house, wasn't he, the pan-German nationalist, the scion of a Czech family? And I myself, with a clientele in four languages, saw daily how my business flourished. Why should it not continue to do so? I was optimistic.

One morning in the spring of 1938 the Reich that had seemed so far suddenly came very near. From my terrace I could see it across the river. With the annexation of Austria the Reich now spread to the banks of the Danube.

In the autumn, when the leaves on the trees along the Danube had turned but not yet fallen, the Reich began to spread in other directions, spilled over into the Sudetenland of Czechoslovakia. President Benes resigned and fled the country. Slovak politicians, seizing their chance, met in Sillein and issued a manifesto proclaiming the autonomy of Slovakia within the Czechoslovakian state. I happened to be in Deutsch-Proben on business at the time, very close to Sillein, but it was not until my return to Pressburg toward the end of October that I heard a detailed account of all these events — from Franz Karmasin, who since the previous year had been an occasional guest in my house.

Karmasin was close to the new Slovakian government. Dr. Tiso, the priest who had become prime minister, had just appointed him chargé d'affaires for the ethnic German minority in Slovakia. Karmasin had had a rapid career; he was already *Volksgruppenführer*. Throughout the autumn he was busy organizing a new volunteer guard group, to be known as the FS, which was conceived very much on the model of the SA and the SS that had long been in existence in the Reich. I congratulated him on his appointment and all his new plans, which would surely benefit German interests in Slovakia, but I remember having to hurry away to the hospital where my wife was in labor with our second child. In retrospect I see that I must have been unusually preoccupied with private matters, business and family, throughout the crucial months of September and October. Thus it came as a shock when all the windows of my retail store were smashed in the course of violent anti-Jewish demonstrations that swept through Pressburg on the night of the third of November. I protested loudly that I was not a Jew — I was not, of course, but ironically my wealth had led me to be taken for one.

On March the fourteenth of the following year (a fateful day for me — my extradition to Czechoslovakia took place exactly eight years later) German troops occupied the country. Bohemia and Moravia were designated a German protectorate; Slovakia presented itself to the world as an independent state, but only four days later Tiso signed a treaty in Vienna that degraded the new republic to an appendage of the Reich, making a mockery of all its claims to independence. Slovaks who had tolerated German intrusions so long as they had served their own political interests discovered anti-German feelings for the first time. I took note of all these important changes, came to the conclusion that so far as I was concerned nothing much had changed for the time being, and resumed negotiations on a very large order which the agent of a road-building machinery company confidentially told me was for the Reich — enormous quantities of shovels, cramp-irons, assorted tools, and machinery. I had to go to Prague for the negotiations and I was accordingly not informed about a new regulation that the Slovak government issued on April thirtieth in Pressburg. The Jews in Slovakia, the regulation ordered, would be allowed to continue management of their businesses only on condition that they agreed to accept fifty-one percent Slovak participation. In this way the government hoped to reduce the preponderance of Jewish capital in the economy of the new republic. In the normal course of things I would have discussed the implications with my Jewish colleagues, but as a result of my having boycotted Jewish nominations for the lodge of the Pressburg free-masons in the previous year the leaders of their business community and the firm of Pallehner were still estranged. I had objected not to the Jews themselves but to their exploitation of the society, as I saw it, for private business purposes. For the time being I was in any case much too busy organizing the acquisition of really immense quantities of shovels and machines and arranging for their transport to destinations in the north along the borders of Silesia, which under the circumstances admitted of only one interpretation. I was accordingly less surprised than most people when in the late summer of that year German tanks began to roll over the border into Poland along roads built with machines and shovels that the firm of Pallehner had helped to supply.

The war brought me good business. Without being a profiteer, I undoubtedly profited from the war. Equipped with my third, Slovakian citizenship, living in one of the Reich's satellite countries, neither occupied nor at war, and quietly beginning to assume those privileges that accrued for the ethnic Germans in Slovakia, I continued to lead the warm, well-appointed, securely provincial life in Pressburg that I had led before the war. I was now the sole representative in Slovakia of some of the largest industrial concerns in the Reich, such as Thyssen and Mannesmann, buying and selling on behalf of the Slovakian industry. From a later point of view, however, my activities in the iron trade would appear to be less important than the directorships I held in half a dozen other concerns, in particular my post on the board of the Bank of Dresden.

I had been instrumental in bringing this bank to Slovakia in order to reduce the dependence of local German craftsmen and tradesmen on the virtual monopoly of Jewish-Hungarian capital. It was a strategic move, which at the time did not appear to be controversial. With hindsight, however, it could be construed as part of that anti-Jewish program, increasingly comprehensive and sinister, that the so-called clerical-fascist government of Slovakia began to put into effect in 1940. For Hitler this program had not gone fast or far enough. In July of that year President Tiso succumbed to pressure from the Reich and dropped Durcansky, who had doubled as minister of the interior and of foreign affairs, from his government. The vacant posts were occupied by Mach and Tuka respectively, both the approved nominees of the Reich. Tiso and the Slovaks had wished to temporize over the Jewish question, not out of any great love for the Jews or respect for the rights that they were still granted under the constitution, but because too prompt a withdrawal of the Jews from the economic life of the country carried the risk of their replacement by Slovakian Germans. But expropriation of the Jews only served the national interests if the Jewish made way for Slovak entrepreneurs. From the point of view of the Slovak separatists the Aryanization of the economy was desirable not because it would remove the Jews but because it would break up the staunch Hungarian loyalties that the Jews still preferred to Slovakian patriotism. Thus Aryanization was primarily an aspect of Slovakian nationalism, and all Slovaks, not just Slovak capitalists, were to be its principal beneficiaries. When the so-called Jewish Code (modeled on the precedent of Nuremberg) was brought before the Slovakian Assembly that autumn it was not surprising, then, that only the leader of the Hungarian minority, Count Esterhazy, voted against it. As for the rest, not only the champions of the Reich but also Slovaks and ethnic Germans who were not of Nazi persuasion — all had their own ax to grind and assented to the suppression of the Jews.

For some time I had been aware of the existence of the Jewish Laws without knowing in detail what provisions they contained. Many of the provisions were prohibitions, and as the fact of someone not doing something is not inherently likely to draw much attention I found that I could still walk out and form the impression that Pressburg's Jewish community of fifteen thousand lived pretty much as it had always done. The Hlinka Guard, forerunner of Karmasin's FS, had put up some foolish signs in cafés to discourage Jewish customers, but these had soon been removed by the police. But then I found to my annoyance that certain of my acquaintances would no longer be able to visit me — Jews were forbidden to enter non-Jewish homes. They would also not be able to call me — Jews were forbidden to use the telephone. They were not allowed to drive cars or bicycles, to be out on the streets after nine o'clock at night, to study at Slovakian colleges, to keep their passports, or to be in possession of fishing equipment: the laws comprised that sinister blend of trivial prohibitions and the infringement of fundamental rights.

During the second half of 1941 the first people began to appear in my office with requests for help. President Tiso had reserved himself the right to exempt individual Jews who were considered indispensable in public life from the provisions of the Jewish Laws. Mostly they were people who played an important role in the Slovakian economy.

Although I was not personally in a position to issue letters of protection, as some of my callers believed, I could at least furnish them with testimonials and arrange the necessary contacts. Most of the presidential letters of protection were issued by the Ministry for Economic Affairs, where I had excellent connections. I knew the minister Medricky quite well. Thus I was able to help the two daughters of an old acquaintance of the family, Colonel Fischer, when they lost their jobs, as the majority of Jews did, and were threatened with deportation. In their case I intervened personally in an interview with the minister, but I never learned the outcome of many of the petitions I was asked to pass on. There were also Jews and Slovaks who came to me asking for jobs, but it had long been a principle of the firm to give precedence to ethnic Germans. I very seldom made exceptions.

When the deportation of the Jews from Slovakia began in 1942 I believed, as did the Jews themselves, that their eventual destination would be Palestine. Rumors of a resettlement of the Jews, whether in Poland, Abysinnia, Madagascar, or Palestine, had been circulating for years. Somehow one had grown accustomed to the idea that it was necessary for the Jews to be resettled. The matter was already decided. But although the deportation of the Jews infringed the rights that the constitution of the republic still guaranteed national or religious minorities, the Jewish Code notwithstanding, there was never any discussion of rights. There were protests from Slovak bishops, but the protests had no effect. Throughout the year of 1942 the deportations continued. Members of the FS, Karmasin's paramilitary organization, assisted the police in confiscating property and arranging transports — I saw them myself in the streets. But I raised no objections, did not even have any serious doubts. Nobody raised objections. The entire non-Jewish population of Pressburg looked on, detached, even indifferent.

In the space of about six months Slovakia's community of eighty thousand Jews almost entirely disappeared. The transports to unknown destinations were suspended in the autumn of 1942. From the Fischer sisters I heard rumors that the representative of the Holy See in Pressburg had intervened with the government because of incidents involving Jewish transports in the Lublin area. The rumors were not substantiated and I heard no more of the matter.

The management of my business took up an increasing amount of my time. Trade flourished, but was no longer expanding; the curve had begun to flatten out. I welcomed the publicity given to my tile factory in Deutsch-Proben by a visit of President Tiso. The visit was fully reported in the Slovakian press; a photograph of the president on the platform where he gave an address showed me standing in the background. But my hopes that the president's visit might lead to government contracts were disappointed. Indeed, relations between the Slovaks and the local German population in general had begun to deteriorate conspicuously from about the time that the Reich's armies ceased to advance and the fortunes of war turned. Night raids on the homes of ethnic Germans and Slovak collaborators caused growing unease. I found my work force increasingly depleted by the conscription of the *Volksdeutsche* into an organization that now, too late, was revealed to me as the perpetrator of the most shocking crimes. An apprentice home on leave from sentry duty in a camp in Poland could not understand why prisoners still attempted to climb over fences right under his nose even when they knew he had orders to shoot them. The boy had been taught machine tooling at my firm. He didn't know what to do. I did not know either. An uprising had just started in Banska Bystrica, deaths had been reported from Deutsch-Proben, where my family was staying, I could get them out only just in time. For the next month we sat tight in Pressburg. The Slovak uprising was put down. The air was full of accusations and counteraccusations, rumors, confusion, treachery. My belief in the final victory of the Reich crumbled. Nothing held anymore. My deputy vanished overnight, his son had joined the partisans; my warehouse was broken into, I found the kilns in the Deutsch-Proben factory cold. Suddenly I ceased to have a business at all. My only remaining duty was to my family. It was reported that the Russians would soon reach Presov in eastern Slovakia. One early morning, in January 1945, I left Pressburg with my family and as much of my household as would fit into two of my delivery trucks, and drove west across the border.

Behind the Bakery

B RATISLAVA two years later had not changed. On the way from the station to police headquarters the bus with the fifteen prisoners drove around the square where my shop stood. Everything was the same, no gaps, no ruined buildings; even the name painted in a frieze above the shop had remained as it was. For Slovakia it had been a good war.

It was early evening when we arrived at police headquarters. We stood waiting in a long dark hall for over an hour. At last a police officer appeared and began to call out names. The men were led off one by one up a flight of stairs at the end of the corridor. Sellner was the first to go. I wondered if I would ever see him again.

At this moment someone tapped me on the shoulder. I turned and saw a young man, who put his finger to his lips and made signs that I should follow him. He slipped back noiselessly into the shadows from which he had emerged, looked around again, nodded, gestured, set off down a corridor. I followed and caught up with him.

"I'm the secretary of the chief of police," said the young man rapidly. "In the first room on the left past the steps you will find your brother-in-law. He has been expecting your arrival and asked me to arrange a meeting. I am a friend of his. I shall be waiting outside. You have only ten minutes!"

I opened the door and found myself in a small office. My brother-in-law got up from a chair beside the door and embraced me warmly.

"Joseph!"

"Ladislav! How on earth did you get in here?"

"Ah, Stefan — he owed me a good turn. And when I told him you were a freemason, that clinched it."

"Not anymore. That's a long time back. But how's Anna?"

"Anna's fine. She's sent you some food — you can't take it with you, so eat now while I tell you the news. First: tomorrow you will be moved from here to the district court prison, where you will be committed for trial. It will be less easy to visit you there and of course impossible to talk freely. So I had to see you tonight. But don't worry — there won't be a trial. They'll be sending you back — that may take time — don't despair! I've spoken with your wife — yes, she's well, the children too, they send their love — and she's doing everything she can to get this terrible business sorted out. Your extradition was ordered by mistake."

"By mistake!"

"On the last day that you were in Dachau the Americans had authorized the extradition of fifteen men. It seems that one of these men was a high Czech official from Prague who had collaborated with the Germans under the protectorate. It was certain that he would be sentenced to death on his return to Prague. Well, he had very influential connections in the West — he had something to do with British military intelligence. Anyway, he just managed to slip his head out of the noose. But by that time the transport of fifteen men had been authorized, the Czechs notified, all the formalities completed. That's where you came in. They were short of a man. They needed a fifteenth man."

"Why?"

"Because fifteen was the number they had marked down in the extradition papers. That's how they think in the army. It would save everyone a lot of trouble."

"Trouble, for Christ's sake!"

I recalled the scene instantly: the snowy strip of land between the barracks and the fence, the man walking away from the truck between two Czech guards whose face had seemed familiar. It *was* familiar: one of the faces around a table at the ministry in Prague in the spring of 1939: picks and shovels for roads to Poland.

"Why me?"

"You were there. And perhaps they counted on your being sent back."

"It doesn't sound much like a mistake to me. It sounds like a deliberate plan."

There was a knock at the door.

"Stefan," said my brother-in-law, grasping my hand, "time for you to go. Keep your spirits up. You'll soon be home. How will the family manage without you? Wife and four children —"

"Three."

"She's expecting the fourth in November."

"What! She's pregnant?"

"She's pregnant. A child to remember you by —"

There was no time for any more questions. My brother-in-law disappeared down the corridor in one direction, Stefan gripped my elbow and hurried off with me in the other. He knocked on a door. It slid open. Another corridor, endless corridors, completely dark. Stefan stopped at a second door, whispered through the grille, the door was opened, he pushed me through and turned back, the door was locked behind me, and a minute later I found myself alone in a cell.

I hardly slept that night. The light remained on in my cell. I lay on my side with my face to the wall and my collar pulled up over my eyes. My brother-in-law Ladislav, news from home! My heart leaped up and shrank. How would my wife manage alone with four children? I must get home! Committed for trial tomorrow. Don't despair. They send their love. Transport of fifteen men.

"Why me?"

"They needed a fifteenth man."

I dozed. Later I walked up and down.

The following morning, ordered out into the corridor to report to the guard, I found that only seven of the fifteen men from the original transport were left. Oberle and Peters were still there, five others whom I knew only by sight. Sellner had gone.

This time, for some reason, we were told our destination: we would be transferred to the district court prison, where we were to be committed for trial.

After a short march through the streets of Bratislava we reached a large modern building four or five stories high. The reception procedures were now thoroughly familiar: the identification of the prisoners, stamping and signing of commitment papers, escort to washrooms where we undressed, showered, were disinfected and given a brief medical examination. Naked we stood in line at a counter to receive our prison clothes and signed a chit confirming that we had identified our personal belongings. The clothes, money, wristwatch, ring, and the few personal articles that my wife had packed for me when I left home that morning in March had traveled independently from Dachau to Pilsen, briefly surfaced there, made their own way farther to police headquarters in Bratislava and now to the district court prison. There was cruelty and injustice, men might be beaten and hanged, but a prisoner's registered belongings were treated with a strange scrupulousness. They would always be waiting for him, intact, wherever and whenever he emerged from prison life. Only one article regularly disappeared: the identification papers of prisoners who had been sent over from the West.

When I pushed my pile of belongings across the counter and signed the ledger I felt that I had therewith taken leave of my private life for an indefinite length of time. It was as if I had shed a skin. I was left nothing that was my own.

We were marched up to the third floor and halted in a large, domed, circular hall from which half a dozen corridors led off like spokes from the hub of a giant wheel. Before the seven of us were separated there was time for a brief impression of stone floors, white walls, a narrowing of perspective and loss of light toward the end of the spoke-like corridors. I was marched by the warder into one of these white tunnels until we reached the well of the stairs. The corner cell — this was my destination.

The cell was much cleaner than the one in Pilsen. Judging by the smell it must have only just been whitewashed. The cell was also smaller — five paces. In Pilsen it had been five and a half. Later I realized that pacing out a cell was an unreliable method of measuring it, because during the months of confinement my natural pace had become quite a bit smaller. I learned to measure cells by precise steps, the length of the foot from heel to toe.

Long periods of confinement brought shrinkage in other ways. Thus I came to devote my full attention to the study of a fly that had the charity to live for a week with me in my cell. For the first time in my life I began to observe detail, because there was nothing but detail to observe. I would spend the first few days in a cell scrutinizing the walls for evidence of its previous occupants. Legends inscribed with a bedspring might remain legible under several coats of whitewash. Most of the messages seemed to have been left by priests or men of strong religious beliefs. In my new cell, on the ceiling directly above my head, I deciphered the exhortation *Domine, in te speramus.* I could not read it when I lay on my bunk, but I knew that it was there; and for some reason that consoled me. Under the window another hand — according to the warder it was the hand of Dr. Tiso, who had allegedly spent some time in this cell during his trial — had scratched the famous line from Dante's *Inferno: lasciate ogni speranza voi ch'entrate!* But I did not think Tiso's religious convictions would have allowed him to admit that one should give up all hope.

At this time I still had hope, around my heart there was still a sense of assurance, a warmth, that the visit of my brother-in-law had given me. Now that my wife was expecting a child the future seemed much clearer. I could face it confidently, knowing that whatever else might be in store it would bring us the happiness of this child. I would be committed for trial but not tried, Ladislav had said. Here in Bratislava I still had many friends and already, in these first few days, had benefited from a conspiracy of kindness, little acts that always had to remain anonymous. Thus I had woken up one morning to find a new pair of boots in my cell — I did not find out how or from whom.

The window of my cell looked out onto a yard where supplies for the prison were unloaded. Some of the firms under contract to the prison were familiar to me; the names were painted across the side of the vans. I watched how frequently they came, what loads they delivered, estimated the value of deliveries and their weekly turnover. A businessman does that quite naturally. And making calculations soothed me, figures normalized my mind.

This yard and the corner of a building on the other side, where women prisoners were accommodated, offered a variety of distractions. For a couple of days a group of prostitutes lived in a cell directly opposite my wing. They posed provocatively at the windows, shouting taunts across the yard to the male prisoners. During one such exchange of ribaldries I was astonished to hear women's voices singing a hymn — subdued and unsteady at first, then filling the yard with full-voiced, incongruous harmony. It was a choir of nuns, who by a gross coincidence happened to be interned in a cell just across the way from the prostitutes. For a moment the prostitutes were shocked into silence, but then, enraged, they started to bawl obscene songs in which the voices of the melodious nuns were soon completely submerged.

But the yard and the buildings on the other side formed part of a world to which I very soon felt I had ceased to belong. My cell had another window that was of much more immediate interest to me: the blind hatch that allowed a glimpse into the corridor when meals were passed into my cell three times a day. Not only meals: this was where I daily, hourly, expected my fate to appear. I had closely examined this blind wooden window, through which everything on which my existence depended would reach me, and had made an important discovery: that the window was not in fact blind, that whenever I chose to I could give it eyes, with the help of a straw from my pallet. Since the hatch fitted imperfectly over the opening, a piece of felt had additionally been hung over it to cover up a chink on one side. The felt required to be prodded no more than a fraction to allow me a partial view of the corridor, with little risk of being detected from outside.

Through this chink between hatch and door I became acquainted with the realities of life in the district court prison, for from the corner cell I could watch the landing and part of the stairs between the second and the fourth floors. The stairs were hardly frequented by day; it was at night that interrogations usually took place, apparently on the second floor, for prisoners always went down, from my own corridor and from the floor above. They were fetched late in the evening and returned in the early morning. Interrogations invariably affected prisoners for the worse. Men who had walked down on their own legs were dragged back upstairs by the arms. The landing and stairs were often swabbed at night. Much of what happened in prison happened when it was dark; the torture that preceded confessions, the confessions that preceded hangings, and the hangings themselves.

Condemned men were housed in a separate block, but they were not completely isolated from the rest of us who were still awaiting trial. After the first few weeks of solitary confinement without privilege of exercise I was allowed to walk out in one of the prison yards. On the first day out in the yard I recognized an old acquaintance of mine, Heubl, a Catholic priest whose parish had been Deutsch-Proben. Prisoners could choose their own partners, so for several weeks, walking in circles around the yard, hands on back, I was able to take my exercise with Heubl and hear his story.

Heubl had been found guilty of treason and sentenced to death the previous year. At the time I met him he had been waiting for his execution for eighteen months. After two years his sentence was commuted to life imprisonment.

Heubl and I were the same age, we were both former Slovakian citizens of German nationality, both of us had close ties to the same ethnic German community in central Slovakia. For these reasons I naturally took a special interest in his case. The extreme severity of his punishment made clear to me how serious my own situation was.

Heubl had been a political priest, like many priests from

the Hauerland, where a decision to enter the church was likely to be influenced as much by worldly as by purely religious considerations. In a poor country like Slovakia the fact of having a priest in the family meant an insurance, should the times become even harder than they already were, against total destitution. Heubl was in this tradition. He had agitated for the rights of his German parish community, its language and culture, not only from the pulpit but in the Slovakian Assembly, to which he was elected as a member of the Carpathian-German Party. His membership in a party that had ideologically been allied to the Sudeten German cause and thus also to the National Socialists in the Reich had counted heavily against him when he was arrested after the war. Unquestionably, he had identified with the ambitions of the Reich where these had coincided with the interests of the German minority in Slovakia. On these grounds he was found guilty of collaboration and treasonable acts against the Czechoslovakian state, and in 1946 he was sentenced to death.

During the eighteen months that had passed since his trial Heubl's certain span of life never exceeded three or four days at a time. Hangings took place on Tuesdays and Fridays, but for condemned men the critical days were Mondays and Thursdays; if on either of these days they were given a medical checkup then it meant execution on the following day.

Heubl bore up under this ordeal with an astonishing fortitude that I felt was only in part attributable to the strength he derived from his religious convictions. He made a strange confession. He was angry that he was afraid, he said. Time and again he had thought that he was prepared for death, time and again his fear of death had showed him that he was not. He seemed to despise the instinct of self-preservation. I got the impression that his resolution in the face of death testified less to the power of his faith than to stubbornness and bigotry. Although I admired Heubl I did not like him. He confronted death with the same inflexibility and tyranny of the will with which he had confronted life.

I learned from him that when the morning coffee was brought around the cells later than usual on a Tuesday or Friday it meant that there had been a hanging. Executions were carried out in a small inner courtyard referred to as "behind the bakery." The building facing onto the courtyard contained not only the bakery but the kitchens, where prisoners helped to prepare breakfast. These preparations could not begin until the execution was over, with the result that on hanging mornings the coffee arrived late.

There were men who allegedly had to wait even longer than Heubl for their execution. The most notorious case was that of Rösch and Porsch, two former SS men who were executed almost three years after they had been sentenced.

Hangings were carried out so frequently at this time that they became a commonplace of prison life, but we were nonetheless deeply shocked by the death of Ludin. Ludin had been the Reich's envoy in Pressburg from 1941. He was tried concurrently with the former *Obergruppenführer* and Waffen SS general Höfle, who had been in command of the German troops in Slovakia during the uprising in 1944. Höfle, as a man, enjoyed little sympathy from his fellow prisoners; his case was considered hopeless. But Ludin was widely respected, by the Slovaks as well as the Germans, for the integrity and courage with which he had defended Slovakian interests against the increasingly predatory Reich. Even during the war this had won him the reputation of being more the envoy of Slovakia in Berlin than the Reich's envoy in Pressburg.

I never spoke to Ludin, but I knew that he was in a cell on the floor above me between Höfle and the Bishop of Zips, Vojtassak. I passed him in the corridor one morning, very pale. A few days later the coffee arrived two hours late. According to rumors I heard in the yard there had been several executions that morning and there had been some "technical delay." In Leopoldov I later shared a cell with the man who had hanged Ludin. Unwisely he boasted to his cellmates that he had contrived the hanging in such a way that the condemned man had survived the fall by ten minutes. The hangman-turned-thief soon regretted his boast, whether true or not, because we gave him a terrible beating.

I suppose there were not many men who awaited death with the same fortitude as Heubl, or who, when the time had come, accepted it as nobly as Ludin. I suppose many more must have died like Schwanzer, the furrier, whose shop stood behind the Martinsdom and whose brother had worked for years in my firm. Schwanzer had been conscripted into the Waffen SS at the beginning of 1944. He had fought against Slovak partisans and was assigned guard duty on some of the last transports that had left Slovakia for Theresienstadt, Auschwitz, and Sachsenhausen — eleven transports, it was stated at his trial, involving over twelve thousand persons.

One night in the autumn of 1947 a warder came to my cell with a request for my cooperation, as he put it, in a difficult matter. The prisoner Schwanzer, who had been tried and condemned to death the previous week, was to be executed the following morning. The prisoner had declined to eat the valedictory dinner to which a condemned man was entitled, but he wished to make use of his privilege to request whatever the prison authorities were in a position to put at his disposal. He had requested to see me. I had known him for many years and had been particularly close to his brother. The warder asked me if I was prepared to spend Schwanzer's last night with him in his cell. I agreed.

I followed the warder up the stairs to the floor above. I could hear Schwanzer raving long before we reached his cell. His shouts were audible all the way down the corridor. When the door was opened I found him standing under the window, white-faced, back to the wall, shrieking "Where is God! Where is God!" I went up to him and put my hand on his shoulder to try to calm him. His neck shot out at the touch, stretched rigid. Heat came off his body, his clothes were damp, he stank of urine. "Schwanzer," I said, "sit down and let's talk." But he couldn't talk, seemed only able to scream, had lost control of his glands, stood open-mouthed with streaming shoes, his whole body, his whole being busy with fear, excreting fear from his bowels and the pores of his skin. "Your brother," I began, and for a moment this seemed to bring him to his senses. His head slumped. "Jews," he croaked, "what did I do to the Jews?" He stiffened, his neck shot out. "I did nothing to the Jews! Where is God! Where is God!" The terrible dirge resumed. There was no longer anything I could do, nothing I could say that would reach him. After a quarter of an hour the warder mercifully unlocked the door and brought me back to my cell.

The following morning, a Tuesday morning, the coffee arrived late, cold coffee, Schwanzer's coffee, that was how I knew he had died, that was his only epitaph.

Schimkov's Notes

MANY members of the government of the former Slovakian republic could be seen at this time in the yard of the district court prison. On my daily walks I recognized Mach and Medricky, ministers of the interior and the economy respectively, Pruzinsky, the finance minister, Julius Stano, the minister of transport, Koso, a former top official in the Ministry of the Interior, and many others whose faces I did not know but whose names were familiar. President Tiso and his deputy Tuka had already been executed. Others, like Durcansky and Karmasin, who had escaped abroad, were sentenced to death in their absence. Several prominent members of the German community were also there — Dr. Gold, police attaché at the German embassy, and Fritz Fiala, editor of the Pressburg paper *Grenzboten,* whom I knew well.

No progress had been made in my own case. Months had already passed. I was visited several times by Dr. Jamnetsky, a former acquaintance from prewar days, whom my brother-in-law Ladislav had engaged as my lawyer. My wife's mother, who still lived in Bratislava, agreed to advance part of her daughter's inheritance to pay for the costs of my defense.

I say: no progress had been made in my case — but I

still had no idea if there was a case against me at all. In late June, a couple of months after I had been committed for trial, I was brought before the examining magistrate, Dr. Tellek, an elegant Jewish lawyer who had lived a few houses down the road from us until his disappearance at the outbreak of the war. I now learned that he had survived the war in exile abroad. I asked him on what grounds I had been extradited.

"The question of your properties must be settled," he said. "Now that you are no longer a Czechoslovakian citizen your properties would normally be forfeited to the state, but it appears that your wife has part ownership. She has retained her citizenship in this country, which complicates the issue, if only formally. . . . I admit that this matter could have been arranged without your personal appearance."

"Then why was my personal appearance required?"

Tellek shrugged.

"At the moment it's impossible to say just why. I can only surmise. The definition of collaboration is very flexible. Throughout the war you were a leader of the German business community here. Apparently you have been identified in a photograph with Tiso. Under present circumstances that alone is enough to justify a thorough examination of your case, even if we have no specific grounds for indictment. So far as the property issue is concerned I have been authorized to make you an offer: if you are prepared to stay in this country as a Czechoslovakian citizen and to assist in the reconstruction of our industry, then I can assure you that it will not be long before you are a free man."

"What about my family?"

"Your family would join you here."

"And if I refuse your offer?"

"It depends what results the investigation of your case

brings to light. The investigation may take some months. Should we decide there are no grounds for prosecution, you would then be allowed to return home."

I turned Dr. Tellek's offer down. Two weeks later, at a hearing that I did not attend, ownership of my properties was transferred to the state. The complications of which Tellek had spoken had apparently not proved to be much of an obstacle. Until this time, despite my two-year absence from the country, I remained the nominal owner of my business, and documents granting jurisdiction in any matter related to it had to be brought to my cell for my signature.

Although this first appearance before the examining magistrate failed to clarify my situation, it did bring me relief from one constant source of anxiety. After their first interrogation prisoners were entitled to receive and write letters. At last I could write home, give a sign of life! And I now began to watch the blind window onto the corridor with a new interest. Once every few weeks the hatch would be opened and a letter tossed in. Thus I learned that my wife and the children were well, that somehow they managed, that a normal life went on outside.

The news that reached me through Dr. Jamnetsky, however, became gradually more discouraging. For months he had buoyed me up on schemes, rumors, hopes; an appeal from my wife to the responsible minister had been conveyed to the Czech authorities via the official channels; there were indications that I would definitely return home in August; I was to be tied into arrangements for the repatriation of General Höfle, in a vain attempt to save his life; I was to be reunited with my family in Dresden and then brought secretly over the border. Nothing came of all these plans. In the second half of 1947 the porous border between East and West was gradually being sealed up. The fronts hardened. Jamnetsky brought a new word with him on his visits to the prison: the cold war. Hope began to recede. Jamnetsky's waiting strategy, which assumed a gradual improvement in the Democrats' bargaining power after their success in the elections of the previous spring, turned out to be wrong. Let us not press for the trial, he advised, public opinion is hostile, wait till the climate improves. But throughout 1947 the climate rapidly grew worse.

In the prison yard I saw fewer and fewer of the old faces. The first wave of prisoners to occupy the prisons and the courts, German war criminals and their Slovak collaborators in what was now termed a clerical-fascist state, had disappeared under a second wave of old-guard Communists, insubordinate priests, and Social Democrats who had become the new enemies of the state. The rapidity with which these elements began to fill the cells of the district court prison probably allowed us inside prison to discern more clearly than a free observer outside in what direction the tide of power had begun to flow. There had been warning signs earlier, but their significance had not been read. They had not been read by Ota Obuch for one, from whom I learned of Czechoslovakia's withdrawal, under Soviet pressure, from the Marshall Conference earlier that summer, when only a few months afterwards we sat together on prison benches, pasting paper sacks in which we secretly wrote messages to the outside world.

Obuch was the secretary of the Democrat Jan Ursiny, deputy prime minister in a succession of governments since the end of the war. In September a department of the Ministry of the Interior had exposed "conspiracies against the republic" in Sillein and Pressburg, in which leading officials of the Democratic Party were allegedly involved. Obuch was among those charged with having played a central part in the conspiracy. The arrest of these prominent party members was the prologue of the bitter struggle between Democrats and Communists that escalated during the following months. For Obuch, this struggle lay on the surface of a deeper enmity between Czechs and Slovaks. In Slovakia the Communists had won less than a third, the Democrats almost two-thirds, of the vote in the elections of the previous year. Compared with the result in Bohemia and Moravia, where the Communists had outclassed their political rivals, in Slovakia they had been humiliated. From then on their policy of support for a relatively independent Slovakia was replaced by the centralist doctrine of Prague. They were suspicious generally of Slovakian separatism, which, as very recent history had shown, was prepared to collaborate even with a fascist power in order to achieve its ambitions; and they were suspicious in particular of its political leaders, whose graduation to the Democratic Party from membership in conservative-agrarian, clerical-nationalistic associations before the war had not been forgotten.

In prison, awaiting trial, I felt like a relic from the past, far removed from all these events in the world outside, but I learned from Jamnetsky that, on the contrary, they had already begun to have an immediate effect on my case. The prosecution intended to bring charges against me as a capitalist collaborator with the fascist powers. My trial was to be exemplary, complementing those trials against Nazi industrialists that had already taken place in the West. There was no longer any chance of repatriation, for my case could now serve new political interests.

During six months in prison I had been summoned to see the examining magistrate only once. Toward the end of 1947 these summonses became more frequent, but it was no longer Dr. Tellek whom I was taken to see. I never saw or heard of Tellek again. Perhaps he had himself been dislodged by the same political interests that now wished to appropriate my trial — I don't know. At any rate, in the chair behind Tellek's desk sat a new man by the name of Schimkov.

Schimkov was a shrewd, secretive man who never revealed anything about himself. I heard he had been a timber merchant, but where he came from, what he felt and thought, where he stood politically, all this remained a mystery throughout the ten or twelve months of our association. This secretiveness belonged to Schimkov's technique. It made him seem omniscient. Other prisoners had warned me to pad my kidneys with a towel whenever I was summoned to an interrogation, but Schimkov never maltreated me, often did not even want to see me at all. He sent me notes, on which was scrawled a sentence or just a word.

The first note arrived in my cell in early December. Two names were written on it, *Karmasin* and *Carpathian-German Party*. The warder who brought the note gave me paper and pencil and told me I was to write answers to the examining magistrate's questions by the following morning. "What questions?" I asked. "He's just written down two names." But the warder merely repeated his instructions and closed the hatch without offering any further explanation.

"I have plenty of time," Schimkov had said at our first meeting, "your time, not mine." I took his note to mean that he wanted me to write down everything I could remember in connection with the two names, and that it would thus depend on me how much longer I waited for my trial. But if Schimkov thought I had anything to hide, he was wrong. On half a dozen pages I wrote everything I knew. The next morning the warder took the pages away and returned a couple of days later with another note on which Schimkov had written the same names. I assumed he was not satisfied, wanted more. I sat down to think, and with some difficulty managed to cover another page.

Not long after my second answer had been conveyed to Schimkov I was taken to see him. He told me my handwriting had been analyzed by an expert in graphology. The verdict on my character was not good, he said, but he would not disclose any details. Perhaps he was bluffing.

"When did you join the Carpathian-German Party?" he asked.

"I don't remember exactly — in the spring of 1938."

"Why did you join?"

"It was the natural thing to do. It was the party to which all members of the Pressburg German community belonged, because it represented our interests."

"It was later renamed the German Party. Did you ever read through the party statutes?"

"I suppose I must have done."

"What does it say in paragraph three?"

"I don't remember."

Schimkov held up a piece of paper and read: "In its existence, its fundamental views and actions the German Party embodies the National Socialist *Weltanschauung*."

He put the paper on the desk.

"If the NSDAP had been registered in Slovakia, would you have become a member?"

"If membership in the party had been felt by a majority of the German community in Slovakia to symbolize our association with the Reich, then yes, I would. Solidarity was what mattered."

"Would you have taken the trouble to read through the statutes of the party before applying for membership? Would you have remembered them?"

I said nothing. Schimkov made notes.

"When did you first meet Karmasin?"

"In the summer of 1937."

"Where?"

"He came with a friend to a party at my house."

"You knew of Karmasin's close association with Henlein and the Sudeten German movement?"

"It was common knowledge. He was a Sudeten German himself."

"What was your opinion of Karmasin?"

I hesitated.

"He was different from us. . . . He didn't really belong to us."

"Who is us?"

"The Germans in Slovakia, the German community in Pressburg. I didn't like him."

"Then why was he a frequent guest at your house?"

"He had to be invited. He was the political leader of the German community. There was no way around him."

"Was he instrumental in helping to obtain orders for your firm?"

"Not directly."

"But you say there was no way around him. You did not like him, but you cultivated him, because he was indispensable to you as a businessman."

"Looking after the German business interests in Slovakia was naturally a part of his responsibilities. . . ."

"Did you know of his correspondence with Himmler?"

"No. He didn't mention any personal contacts with Himmler."

"But you knew that he was forming a fascist police organization called the FS on exactly the same lines as the SS?"

"Yes. But we knew very little about the SS at the time. We identified with the Reich, but actually it was very remote from us in Pressburg. We were not informed of the exact nature of the events that were taking place in the Reich."

I went away from the interview with Schimkov feeling rather dissatisfied, as if I had not succeeded in giving a very good account of myself. It was true that I had nothing to hide; but I didn't have very much to show either. In the bald question and answer exchanges that became the routine in my sessions with Schimkov there was no place for explanations of that complex historical background in which I had been born and grown up. Fundamental beliefs, like my belonging to Pressburg's German community and my loyalty to it, which I had taken for granted as sufficient justification for all my actions, were suddenly made to appear deeply suspect. I could see the blight of a lost war, whose real fatality had only become clear to me afterwards, beginning to work back retroactively through all the branches and arteries of my life, poisoning it to the core.

Schimkov's questions revealed that he must have a detailed knowledge of my life over the past ten years. He knew as much about me as myself, in some respects even more: he had access to the vast paper memory of my entire business correspondence and all my private papers. From letters and diaries he could determine what I had thought, felt or done on any particular day. His agents, Jamnetsky told me, had collated from all this evidence whatever information he might conceivably want to use to support the charge. Confronted by a mass of knowledge about myself but detached from myself, over which I had no control and Schimkov all, I found I was talking to a person who could see me exactly as I saw myself, but who never shared this view. A sense of self-dissociation set in. I began to question myself.

During this winter of 1947–48 my self-confidence reached

its lowest ebb. I faced the prospect of a very long term of imprisonment, possibly for life. I began to fear that I might never see my wife and family again. In November, had all gone well, she had given birth to our fourth child, but there had been no news from her for months. Permission to write or receive letters had suddenly been suspended for all remand prisoners extradited from Germany. Everything was getting worse — the food, the privileges of exercise, the now almost uninterrupted solitary confinement. This deterioration of conditions inside prison reflected the severity of the growing political crisis outside.

In February the crisis broke. The Democrats were ousted and the Communists began to consolidate power. The in-prison information network continued to function, despite all attempts to suppress it, and with the arrival in the district court prison of several eminent politicians — among them the Democrat Party leader and recent deputy prime minister, Jan Ursiny — became highly topical and reliable. There were still members of parties other than the Communists in the new government, but democratic opposition had now effectively come to an end, and the era of internecine Communist purges began ominously with the unexplained death of Jan Masaryk, the foreign minister, only a few weeks later. According to prison rumors he had been thrown out of the window of a fortress in Prague.

For my part, however, I continued to inhabit an increasingly distant past, reliving in the isolation of my cell events that had taken place five, ten, or fifteen years ago. Instead of letters, I received, sometimes daily, enigmatic notes from Schimkov, questioning names and dates that I thought had long since disappeared from my memory.

This enforced confrontation with the past gradually effaced the present, in which one day had in any case become indistinguishable from another. Awareness of living in the present, of present time itself, submerged for weeks at a stretch. The notes that were passed into my cell on any one day in the present summoned my thoughts back to the corresponding day in the past. Schimkov determined the year, but always in accordance with this symmetry of past and present and the point at which they met, the seam of an anniversary. I found that all days were anniversaries. For three days in March I was visited in my cell by an agent from the Reich who discussed with me the logistics of an order intended for the blitzkrieg in Poland; nine years later to the day we again put our signatures to the agreement and shook hands. At the end of March a shabby Slovak Jew came through the door and asked if I could use an accountant. I was about to go out for lunch with a client and told him to come back the following week. He never did; but I recorded the man in my diary because of his striking resemblance to my brother-in-law. On April 3 I found myself standing once more on the station platform in Sillein, waiting for a train to Pressburg. It was three days before Easter 1942. In a station siding I saw a long goods train with barred cars of the kind used for cattle transport. The cars were covered and boarded up, leaving one slat open for ventilation at the top. A coil of barbed wire stretched across the opening, behind which I saw to my astonishment the faces of children. The faces appeared and disappeared at short intervals. Apparently the children were being held up for a breath of fresh air. I asked one of the station staff what the meaning of this was and he told me it was a transport of Jews. On April 7, four years before I saw the cattle cars at Sillein station (in my cell it was the tenth anniversary), I formally joined the German Party and received again, this time unsmiling, my membership card from the hands of Franz Karmasin personally. This overlapping of remembered events, incongruous only in time, seamless in their logic, took place under the direction of Schimkov's notes. In his patchwork of anniversaries the chronology was suspended, not the logic, which emerged from this process of thematic juxtaposition with hard, bright clarity.

Throughout April and May I continued, in the silence of my memory, to furnish materials for the East European front, to arrange donations from the Pressburg Germans to the war effort of the Reich, to confer with the directors of banks and industrial concerns, financing loans to German craftsmen, facilities for German apprentices, and watching my business, my personal income and status in the local community grow. In honor of my services to the Reich I was awarded the War Service Cross, second class.

With the anniversary of this award, in early June, Schimkov's flow of notes came to an end. The mosaic was complete. It seemed he had reached a decision.

At about this time I received a letter from my wife, the first in more than six months. The sanction on all letters addressed to or from Germany had still not been lifted, but my lawyer, Jamnetsky, thought of a way around this problem. He discovered that correspondence with Switzerland was not forbidden. In Switzerland I had known for years a man called Bubb, the director of a firm that had supplied me with materials before the war. Jamnetsky suggested I send letters to my wife care of Bubb, phrasing the letters in such a way as to mislead the censorship into thinking that my wife was actually living in Switzerland. This ruse worked perfectly: Bubb read between the lines and understood the situation, sent the letter on to Germany with a covering note and forwarded to me from Switzerland the letters he got back from my wife. My wife tailored news of the family and familiar features of our home to Bubb's house in Geneva. In hospital there she had given birth to a son. She and the child were well. But what of me? Had

I already stood trial? When would I be coming home? I was unable to answer most of my wife's questions, not only because of the censor's restrictions, but because I still didn't know the answers myself.

I had now been held on remand, in a total of five prisons and camps, for a period of sixteen months, with no definite prospect of when I could expect my trial to take place or whether there would even be a trial at all. There had been so many false starts that I no longer attempted to hope. But when one morning at the end of June I bent down with a pounding heart to pick up the piece of paper the warder had tossed into my cell I knew that the time had come. It was a note from Schimkov, and I knew that it would be his last: it was a blank note, a white piece of paper.

What lay under the surface of this paper? What question had not yet been asked? What was there left to ask?

Nothing, only an answer of one or two words, in which all other questions cumulated.

After several sleepless nights this answer spelled itself out on the blank piece of paper. It had emerged of its own accord. I could see it on the surface. Reluctantly I traced it with my pencil.

Why did I write this word? What was I guilty of?

A few days later I was taken to see Schimkov. He sat with his hands clasped in front of him on an empty desk.

"I have a certain sympathy with your case," said Schimkov, addressing not me but the desk. "It is a typical case, typical of hundreds of thousands of people now living on the other side of the border who will never stand trial. Pallehner happened to be a little bit more prominent. That's why he is here."

Schimkov raised his eyes from the table and looked me in the face.

"As a businessman you put your services at the disposal

of the Reich, you contributed to the war. But so did the lawyers, doctors, teachers, factory workers, and farmers, so did all Germans, and I don't think that your case is basically different. It is geographically different, so it acquires a different legal tag: you can be accused of collaboration. But in my opinion all Germans were collaborators, because I regard the Reich itself as having been an occupied country. They all share the same moral responsibility. They cannot all be held legally responsible, however, even though the great majority of them are guilty: not of what they did, but of what they failed to do. And not only the Germans — I have no illusions about that. The Czechs in Bohemia and Moravia, the Slovaks here, for example, are for the most part guilty of what they failed to do. They found a compromise, some would say wisely. Relatively peaceful coexistence. Living arrangements mutually compatible. Each person looking after his own interests, acting to his own advantage. This is why everyone has been so eager to denounce the collaborators afterwards. Scapegoats were required, individuals who could be sacrificed in atonement for a not clearly attributable guilt. In some cases the punishments may appear to be unjust. I can understand your opinion that Tiso, as an individual, did not deserve to be hanged."

"During the five years of Tiso's republic not a single person was executed in this country."

"True. He allowed them to be executed elsewhere. But Tiso had to be condemned to death all the same. Why? Because it provided the legitimation to condemn others to death, people who had willfully committed crimes. It also demonstrated to the outside world that the fascist element that had flourished here during the war would be rooted out in earnest. But above all Tiso is exemplary for what he failed to do. He is one of the evaders who can be named, whose omissions can be counted. He failed to take action. Everyone failed to take action. It is easy to isolate and punish willful crimes, but what of willful omissions? Or simply: omissions? It is legitimate to execute Tiso, because he traded the lives of more than fifty thousand Slovak Jews in exchange for the security of his republic; but what of the two or three million citizens of that republic who allowed Tiso to trade the Jews in exchange for their own peace and quiet?"

Schimkov paused, as if expecting an answer to his question, but I had nothing to say.

"Their omissions have gone unrecorded. It is in the nature of omissions to go unrecorded. The recorded, palpable crimes of war are overshadowed by the immeasurably greater number of unrecorded crimes of peace, for which there is not even a name. All crimes, the crimes of war criminals or of the so-called collaborators, recorded and unrecorded, hinge on the fate of the Jews, and in particular on the charge of omission, of having failed to take action. You are — at the very least — among the collaborators."

"Because of what I failed to do?"

"Not only that. I cannot charge you with omissions, but I can charge you with quite a number of actions that contributed indirectly to the death of the Slovakian Jews."

"For example?"

"For example a memorandum dated February 1942, quoting an offer your company made for a limited supply of rails to the Slovakian national railways. I traced this order back to the source and discovered that it had been placed by the Ministry of Transport in connection with what was then called the evacuation of the Jews. I cannot prove that you were aware of this, but it remains a fact that your company supplied two kilometers of rails along which several thousand people were carried toward their death. . . . You made a substantial profit on this order."

I was stunned.

"No, I wasn't aware of it."

"Quite," said Schimkov tonelessly. "For a long time I considered whether or not to specify actions detrimental to the Jewish population under the general charge of collaboration with the Reich. On balance I decided not. Your photograph has now been on display in the synagogues of Bratislava for over a year. No one has come forward to make a denunciation . . . if only because there are very few people left who could. Then there is Novan, or Neumann, the German Jew employed by your company during the critical years of the war. Did you shelter him because he was a German or a Jew? I don't know, so I shall give you the benefit of the doubt, although somewhere, in all your actions, there is a self-seeking motivation. I know you very well now."

"You've chosen to ignore the fact that I saved the life of two Jews."

"Two Jews? Come now, why so coy? You mean the two daughters of Colonel Fischer, whom you saved as a result of that apparently altruistic intervention with Medricky? Was it merely altruistic? You had occasional sexual relations with both sisters throughout the war . . . presumably you kept their correspondence in your business papers at the office so that you would not be found out by your wife. But that does not concern me. These are matters that will not be raised at your second, that is to say, at your official trial. They belong in the undisclosed files of what I call your first trial, which will remain a private matter between the two of us. It has been a trial of your omissions. You have reached your own verdict, which is as I had intended. You may plead differently at your public trial, but the verdict will be the same. On August the sixth the People's Court in Bratislava will hear the official case against Joseph Pallehner. It will find him guilty of collaboration and sentence him to prison for six years."

Schimkov called the guard and I was taken back to my cell.

A week later a gray envelope was posted through the hatch in my door. The envelope contained my official indictment.

It read as follows:

Registered with the court of Bratislava, June 15, 1948
The examining magistrate in Bratislava
I hereby bring

the accusation

against Joseph Pallehner, born on April 29, 1902, in Bratislava, with right of domicile in the same, resident in Munich, merchant, propertied, educated, married, no previous conviction, on remand in the district court prison of Bratislava since April 30, 1947,

that

in Bratislava on April 7, 1938, he voluntarily became a member of the German Party, in the leadership of this party performed the function of an economic adviser and as such was placed by the party on the executive committees and boards of all trading companies in which the Germans took a financial interest, that he placed at the disposal of the party, for an apprentices' fund, the annual income of 100,000 crowns arising from his activities on such committees, and contributed to the German war effort a further 10,000 crowns raised through donations, for which Hitler awarded him the War Service Cross, second class. As an important figure in the nation's economy he gave

therefore

his services to the occupation administration and the fascist government, in order to assist in establishing this government, in maintaining it, thus prolonging the sufferings of the Slovak people, whereby he committed the crime of collaboration, as defined in Paragraph 5, article d, in accordance with which he is declared to be

guilty.

I felt I had been cheated by Schimkov when I read this indictment. It contained a number of errors, in themselves perhaps unimportant, but what had hitherto persuaded me in Schimkov's argument was his grasp of detail, and the significance he elicited from detail. Thus, for example, I had never been in the leadership of the party, let alone an economic adviser to it; neither had I been placed by the party on any executive committees — I had done so in my own right and of my own accord. Apart from such inaccuracies, I resented the tendentious wording of the indictment, its grossly general argument. Somehow it seemed an almost disappointingly trivial, a ridiculous conclusion to have had to wait one and a half years for.

Certainly I had collaborated, but I did not regard myself as guilty of "collaboration"; at least not of the charges raised in the indictment, for I did not consider them to be crimes. The charge that I had prolonged the sufferings of the Slovak people was a mere slogan, which was automatically written into all indictments issued at this time. On the other hand there was no denying that my conscience was not clear regarding a number of matters that had been the subject of the notes exchanged between myself and Schimkov, but which had not been specifically mentioned in my indictment.

Schimkov had foreseen the sophistry of my inner debate, the wriggling between conscience and self-righteousness. And perhaps that was why he took no trouble with the formal indictment — equally anticipating that in my heart I would find my punishment justifiable, even if I pleaded not guilty.

On August the sixth my trial duly took place, I duly pleaded not guilty. Two hundred people attended. It was a public occasion, an act of ritual purification whose course had long since been planned, including the duration of the hearing, which began at nine and ended punctually at four. In just over six hours I was found guilty and sentenced to six years imprisonment. I was now a convicted war criminal.

On the night after my trial I was led down to the basement of the district court prison into an enormous underground cell. Inside this cell stood a smaller, barred construction, apparently a cage, which I was locked into: a cage inside a cell. I remained standing with one hand holding a bar of the cage until my eyes had become accustomed to the dim light; fortunately so, for I soon made out a channel or conduit, about two feet deep, running across the center of the floor of the cage, into which I would otherwise have fallen. The conduit explained the very unpleasant odor that I had noticed the moment I entered the basement: it was a sewer.

Crouching in a corner of the cage, I must have fallen asleep and slumped forward, hitting my head on the floor, for when I awoke I found blood on my face. I thought I could hear sounds, but having often experienced the deceptions to which one became susceptible during prolonged solitude and silence, I at first attributed them to my imagination. When the sounds persisted, however, I got up to see where they came from. I could not make out anything distinctly beyond the faint brownish pallor that a light source on the basement ceiling shed over the cage; nothing but gradually thickening rings of darkness around me. After peering into the darkness for a long time I thought I could see the floor move: not something on the floor, but the entire floor itself. The sewer was disgorging rats, hundreds of rats.

I scrambled hastily up the bars of the cage and watched in horror as the rats swarmed out of the conduit and spilled like a tide across the floor beneath me. The swarm was so dense that the rats sometimes ran across one another's backs. A muted scuffing and pattering, the indescribable sound of a jostling live swarm, like paper being softly crumpled, rose up out of the crawling dark. I don't know how long I clung to the bars above them. I don't know if the rats could not or were not interested to reach me. At any rate they did not attempt to. The swarm passed by underneath me, vanishing into the dark, but it was not until the last whispering agitation had died out that I ventured to come down.

When the warder fetched me out the next morning I was numb with exhaustion and fright, although I had survived the night much better, he remarked, "than most of the fascist rats."

So this was the crude symbolism of my dungeon. Through the same sewer an increasingly large number of rats, whose names changed with their political masters, would drag their way to the fortress of Leopoldov in the following years.

Leopoldov

THE prison in which I was to spend the next few years of my life was a medieval fortress, once used as a monastery and converted into a prison during the eighteenth or nineteenth century. The grim, star-shaped pile was visible from a great distance on the horizon, dominating the landscape, so we had leisure to appreciate it as the train approached. I gleaned my first information about the history of Leopoldov from the man to whom I was handcuffed, General Turanec, former commander-in-chief of the Slovakian army. He had been tried and sentenced to life imprisonment on the same day as myself. By a coincidence of the alphabet I and Turanec were issued successive numbers — 6413 and 6414. He told me that until the war there had never been more than two or three hundred numbered prisoners in Leopoldov. Within a few years the number had risen to over six thousand. "That's progress," he commented dryly. I lost track of Turanec soon after our arrival, but I heard later that he died in the fortress.

All new arrivals were first placed "in quarantine" — solitary confinement under observation — for a couple of weeks, so that the prison administration could form an opinion of the prisoner's character. I must have passed this scrutiny to their satisfaction, for in the autumn of 1948 I finally emerged from solitary and was integrated as an active, normal member into the larger prison community.

Although a gregarious man by nature, I found the transfer into a cell that I shared with sixty other prisoners less easy than I had imagined. Survival problems in solitary were of a quite different nature from those with which I was now confronted. My rudimentary bodily needs, sleep, food, the movement of my bowels — everything was dictated by the requirements of a common routine, as rigid as it was arbitrary, that it took a long time to learn to accept.

The toilet facilities were among the worst impositions. In one corner of the room, behind a loose boarded screen, stood the tin barrel into which we defecated. For the needs of sixty men it was not a large barrel. There was no flush or outflow — when the barrel was full it simply overflowed. Access to the barrel during the peak hours after breakfast and supper was strictly regulated. Each of us came and went at a fixed time, whether he wanted to or not. There were no means of cleaning oneself afterwards.

Every morning two men took it in turns to empty the barrel. It had to be carried down the stairs and out into the yard, where an oxcart waited with an enormous manure container, open at the top, against which was leaned a ladder. Two men somehow had to climb up this ladder, carrying a barrel brimming with excrement, and tip it into the container — a task it was impossible to achieve without some of the contents splashing one's hands and face. I suppose that the indignity to which we were thus subjected was a deliberate part of our punishment, as the prison authorities never took up the suggestions we made for more hygienic methods of disposal.

What a foul business it was! I thought I wouldn't be able to stand it a second time, but by the third or fourth time I was already coming to accept it as part of my life, and after a dozen times it had become as natural as any other prison chore.

We took our turns to wash every morning and evening just as we took it in turns to squat on the board over the barrel. We shared five basins between us, at which we attempted a sort of cleanliness. Perhaps the effort mattered more than the result. Each man could fetch half a liter of water from the corridor in order to wash — not even enough to rinse the basin for the man afterwards. Clean water was thus always poured into filthy basins, washing accomplished no more than the exchange of one's own dirt with the dirt of the next man. Under such conditions I soon realized that the relations between prisoners could not afford to be of a neutral kind; likes and dislikes became much more pronounced than in ordinary life. A man one liked was a man with whom one was prepared to exchange one's dirt. Companionship was essential if one wished to survive.

Every Friday, after we had taken our weekly shower, we could briefly experience the pleasure of being clean, but I found the process by which we were made clean so distasteful that I did not look forward to these Fridays in the way that some of my fellow prisoners did.

As many as eighty or a hundred naked men were herded by the warders into the shower room, locked in and left to themselves for half an hour. The water was turned on outside and piped through sprinkler nozzles, spaced at intervals across the ceiling of the room. It was almost unbearably hot. Perhaps the temperature of the water served as a hygienic precaution, or perhaps it was impossible to regulate. There the men stood, shoulder to shoulder in a cramped space, jostling and elbowing one another under the scalding water. Within minutes the steam surging up from the floor had become so dense that one could not see more than a couple of yards. Soap, hot water, the press of naked flesh and all its unstilled appetites: what happened here each Friday afternoon, whether voluntarily or under coercion, was likewise an inevitable part of prison life, and one did well to shed one's dirt in the company of those one knew and trusted.

In the prison laundry we were issued a new set of clothes for the week: underwear, gray shirt and trousers, two pieces of square cloth (instead of socks) to wrap around our feet. The clothes were reasonably clean, but they were worn, often threadbare, and they never fitted. Every Friday the exchange or barter of clothes that more or less fitted would begin again, but we looked a miserable bunch of scarecrows nonetheless. We had particular problems with the foot cloths, which often wore through and became unusable in the course of the week. There was no alternative but to resort to our shirttails to remedy the deficiency, tearing strips off the bottom with which to bind our feet. These shirts that had been sacrificed in the interests of feet shrank upwards, leaving one's midriff exposed. Sometimes one was unlucky and found one had also received a jacket on which the lower buttons were missing, which in winter meant an unpleasantly cold week.

Cold hands, cold stomach, cold knees — anything was better than cold feet. On work tasks outside in the bitter Leopoldov winters I learned the primacy of my feet, paid attention to their complaints, sacrificed everything for their welfare. When shirts and trouser bottoms had exhausted their surplus we resorted to blankets. In the course of time a generation of blankets likewise began to shrink upwards over shins and knees, vanishing strip by strip into prisoners' boots — sacking, mattress padding, it didn't matter, our feet were a greedy industry that could make use of anything.

Prisoners assigned to the clothes distribution counter were accordingly among the most influential in Leopoldov. For the most part they were common criminals, who often used their monopoly power to make life difficult for the political prisoners. The prison administration tacitly concurred with this system and the abuses to which it led.

By the same token, the political cases were often assigned the most unpleasant tasks. Long spells in the laundry, for example, often proved ruinous for one's health. My time there was mercifully short. The clothes were washed in huge vats containing lye, a corrosive alkaline solution. The steam and foul vapors that drifted up out of these clothes-steeps impregnated the air and scoured one's lungs. During my assignment to the laundry I became acquainted with Tido Gaspar, writer and former propaganda minister under Tiso, who had been laundering prisoners' clothes for the past eighteen months. His flesh had begun to disintegrate. Acid steam had eroded the right half of his face and caused some kind of atrophy in his facial muscles; his face twitched constantly. He was a witty, educated man whose spirit remained undiminished despite the rapid decay of his body. Later I entertained other prisoners with Tido Gaspar's stories when we dug his grave in the cemetery of Leopoldov.

Our common cell — our common room, really, for it was too large to be described as a cell — was like all the other rooms in Leopoldov, of which I was to experience quite a few in the course of my imprisonment. Twenty-five iron bedsteads, each with its straw mattress, straw pillow, and shrinking blanket, were lined up a foot or two apart on either side of the room. In the middle of the room stood benches and tables where we ate our meals and whiled away the evenings and the apparently interminable weekends.

Under the windows of the shorter wall, facing the door, stood another ten bedsteads, making sixty in all. I slept under the window, chilly in winter, but with the advantage of fresh air on summer nights when the room became heavy with the smell of its inmates.

On the wall behind each bed hung a plaque with the prisoner's name, number and term of imprisonment. In my own case, for example: Joseph Pallehner, 6413, six years. I knew of very few cases of less than six years, and many of my roommates were there for life. They scoffed at my six years. "Six years! I could sit that out on half my arse!" This was the standard term of derision for low sentences. Six, ten, and fifteen years were the common sentences. There were two categories of lifers — those whose term was fixed at twenty years, and those, for the most part murderers, whose plaque carried the somber Slovakian inscription *He shall be released through death*. This room, particularly when it was deserted, with its bleak rows of pallets and corresponding wall plaques, bore a striking resemblance to a graveyard, which for those who were waiting to be released through death must have ceased to be a resemblance and become a palpable fact.

My mattress neighbor on one side was a Pressburg grocer by the name of Christoph Welser. He was a corpulent man of about fifty, equipped with a pinkish, shiny complexion by day and a sonorous snore at night, neither of which was in the least affected by the years he spent in Leopoldov. Welser had even less than a half-arse sentence — a mere three years. He claimed he had spent six months on remand in prison without any idea of the charge on which he had been committed. Welser spoke not a word of Czech or Slovak and not until the actual day of his trial, when at last he was supplied with the services of an interpreter, did he find out what was going on, for the authorities took the view that as a citizen of Czechoslovakia it was incumbent on Welser to be able to speak one or the other of its languages. But Welser spoke only German. He was periodically hauled out in front of the examining magistrate and submitted to unintelligible harangues, he attended a preliminary hearing whose subject remained a complete mystery, and in this way managed to spend half a year in prison without becoming any the wiser as to why he was there.

At his trial it astonished him to learn that the court took him to be Franz Karmasin's chauffeur.

"Karmasin must have had a chauffeur by the name of Christoph Welser, you see," he explained to me, "and that was the trouble, because that happens to be my name too. They arrested me thinking I was this other Welser. Imagine! I don't even know how to drive a car. Said so at my trial. You've got the wrong man, I said. But who would believe that? So they made short work of me. Bang bang! Three years for Karmasin's chauffeur!"

Every week Welser filled out a report card with a request for his case to be reviewed on the grounds of mistaken identity, every week it was turned down. He served the full three years.

On the other side of Welser slept Ota Obuch, the secretary of Ursiny, whom I already knew from the district court prison, where we had spent several weeks together pasting paper sacks. At night we were separated less by the body of Christoph Welser than by his snore, which for the first few weeks disturbed our attempts to get to sleep. Welser slept a solid, vegetable, grocer's sleep, the snore yawning in his throat, as inalienable from the sleeping Welser as his shiny complexion from the waking. There was no point in shaking Welser. Sleep reclaimed him instantly. How long that shredded, yawning snore would have continued to plague our nights I do not know, had not Obuch once, in a fit of uncharacteristic impatience, snatched the pillow from under his head. Welser slept on, but his snore, to our astonishment, immediately ceased. This snatched-pillow trick solved the snoring problem permanently.

Obuch called Welser the Burgher of Calais on the left, quite why I do not know. Apparently there was something about Welser that reminded him of one of the figures in Rodin's *Burghers of Calais*. He was a man of stupendous conservatism, and associated with this conservatism was a naivete that only our fondness for Welser prevented from calling foolishness.

"I've been married for many years," Welser once announced solemnly, "but if only I knew what a woman looks like between her legs."

"Come on!"

"No, seriously."

"But you just said you're married, you idiot."

Welser looked at us both reproachfully out of his solemn turnip face. "Surely you're not suggesting that my wife lets me see her naked?"

Such was Welser, the Burgher of Calais on the left. Obuch made charcoal drawings on the floor to explain to him the anatomy of woman, but the Burgher never really believed him.

Obuch made lots of drawings, the most memorable of which was the drawing of a ladder on the wall over his bed. The ladder had twenty rungs, one for each year of his sentence. The bottom rung was marked 1948, the top one 1968.

"Look," explained Obuch to enquirers, "this is my ladder of hope. All I must do is climb it."

My other mattress neighbor was Boros, a professional thief. Boros was a handsome fellow whose love of luxury had made it inevitable that he had always lived above his

72

means. At the age of fourteen he went into apprenticeship with a housebreaker in Budapest. For a few years they were a highly successful team, until one day they were seen breaking into a jeweler's shop and chased by the police through the streets. Boros could run faster than his companion and managed to escape, while his associate, faced with the alternative of being caught or risking a leap into the Danube, opted for the latter and was never seen again. Boros caught a train to Pressburg the same day, where he was unknown to the police and could resume his profession with a clean slate. He mentioned a number of villas he had "done" whose owners I knew. But after a few years he tired of private houses and carried out a raid on a shoe shop. This gave him the idea of opening a shoe shop himself. With a modest starting capital and business stock, furtively acquired from the inventory of his new competitors, Boros moved to a small town about fifty miles from Pressburg and opened his own business. He found that he was less successful at selling shoes than at stealing them; his new business soon had to be subsidized by his former night work. The Slovakian police now began to take a closer interest in his activities, but at this delicate juncture in his career Boros heard of an organization that was anxious to recruit new members, no questions asked, and which was even prepared to grant them a certain immunity. It was in this way that Boros came to join the Waffen SS. A few months later the uniformed thief Boros took part in the purge of the Warsaw ghetto. Later he was assigned guard duty on the transports of Jews in Czechoslovakia. He ran away at the end of the war and went into hiding in Budapest, but his previous history caught up with him. He was extradited and sentenced to ten years.

Boros was one of a clique of Magyars in our room, all of them thieves, even if some of them, like Boros, had been sentenced for other crimes. I took a special interest in this group, partly because I liked to speak Hungarian, partly because I was still sentimental about the old Hungarian monarchy. The leader of the group, and one of the most intriguing personalities in our room, was a sly, soft-hearted old rascal by the name of Csaba.

At the time I met him Csaba was already sixty-five. He had been a regular guest in Leopoldov on and off for the past forty years. Before the war he had served more than a dozen sentences and was now nearing the end of what he had firmly decided should be his last. Altogether he had spent twenty-eight years in prison.

"It's time for Csaba to retire," he announced, "find a new wife, raise a family. Poultry business may be good."

In exchange for cigarettes, buttons, food, and in winter a place by the stove Csaba entertained his fellow prisoners with stories from a repertoire of fifty years of trickery and mischief. He transformed himself into a legend to which we listened spellbound. He had never had any profession other than that of a thief. He was a thief by passion and in accordance with a firm social conviction that wherever he found too much wealth he should take some of it away and spend it or distribute it. Csaba seemed to be genuinely not interested in personal gain, at least not in hoarded gain. He wanted to enjoy life.

Csaba spoke Hungarian and Slovak with a quaint, somewhat archaic diction. He always referred to himself in the third person, perhaps because this provided him with a better vehicle for his stories and a rhetorical margin in which to moralize on the consequences of his actions. He deplored Csaba's mistakes with the same vigor that he praised his cunning. Probably he appropriated a lot of stories that were not his own. They all began with the same preamble — a technique he may have borrowed from his favorite story-book, *Tales of the Arabian Nights*.

"Csaba, my friends, was a thief with a good heart. He never hurt a fly and he took only from those who had to give. Was Csaba a bad man? You may judge for yourselves from the following story.

"At the time of which I am speaking Csaba was still a young thief and had only just taken up his trade. He had come from the country to Budapest and did not know where the rich people lived. How was he to tell the rich houses from the poor houses? By comparison with his own village all the houses in Budapest seemed to be very rich. And once he had got into one of these great houses, how would he ever find where the owner kept his money and jewels? Csaba had never expected such difficulties and was very downcast.

"But wait! In the villa behind these iron gates lived the managing director of some important company. How convenient for a thief that here in Budapest the owners of houses announced themselves on a large brass nameplate outside in the street! It would save Csaba a lot of trouble. He decided that if a man wanted his title put up in the street he would also be likely to buy his wife expensive jewels. The managing director must be a man who liked things to show off. Csaba at once grasped the situation and made up his mind to return the same night.

"Already midnight! Night comes quickly for her favorite thief Csaba. He is over the wall in a trice, breaks a window, waits, listens, climbs quickly into the house. Csaba's tinderbox shows him that he is in the managing director's study. There is his desk, how convenient, it is unlocked. Csaba pulls open the drawers and finds five thousand crowns in cash. A few minutes' work. He does not even bother to look for the wife's jewels. Csaba puts the money in his pockets and climbs back into the street.

"But what a surprise! Two days later there is a big head-line in the Budapest paper. House of managing director broken into, thirty thousand in cash and jewels worth fifty thousand crowns stolen! Great excitement!

"Only the honest thief Csaba knows: managing director is swindling insurance company of seventy-five thousand crowns.

"But what did Csaba do with all the money? He went to eat and drink the managing director's health in a restaurant on the outskirts of Budapest. He paid for half a dozen girls to eat and drink with him and ordered a band of gypsy musicians to play for him the entire night; but without a cymbal player, Csaba liked to play the cymbals himself. He took the cymbals off their stand and placed them on the backsides of naked girls, cymbals on naked flesh, the true sound of Magyar folk music that Csaba loved, all night long until morning came and the managing director's money was spent.

"For the managing director a profitable business, for Csaba an entertaining night with Tokay wine and gypsy music. Now tell me, who was wronged?"

Most of Csaba's stories were stories of Csaba as a young man, still full of hope and an irresistible urge for life. Al-though the aging Csaba had not lost his vitality, there was little for which he could hope beyond his poultry, perhaps, and a yearning for a secure family life, which would prob-ably remain a dream. During the last years of his life he had continued to work as a thief, not for excitement and pleasure, as he had done as a young man, and not even in the cause of his quixotic social mission, but merely in order to secure a warm berth during the winter months. Csaba was down and out. He committed calculated offenses of a petty nature, which the courts charitably interpreted as an appeal for help. Every autumn he would be arraigned on some minor charge and sentenced to six months to tide him over the winter.

But Csaba would not admit that he was destitute. He claimed other, more urgent reasons for his return to Leopoldov each year.

"There is a small vineyard by the wall on the south side that Csaba must tend for his friend the prison doctor. I have tended it for many years. What would happen to the doctor's vineyard if Csaba were not there to look after it? It would run wild. All the judges in Pressburg know this very well. When Csaba is brought into court in September each year the judge is already nodding and smiling. 'Ah, the vineyard must be tended. Six months, Csaba!' That is why they send me to Leopoldov and not to the local prison for the less serious offenders.

"And then there is the problem of Csaba's daughters. All my daughters — and as you know, I have three — are whores. Csaba and his daughters live together in the same house, so in the winter months it is better for the daughters if Csaba is not at home. Better for Csaba too. I was at home when the Russians came in 1945. The soldiers rushed into the house and shouted *Dawaj!* as soon as they saw the three girls, but I told them force not necessary, daughters always willing.

"But enough of Csaba's daughters! Tonight I shall tell you a story that happened forty years ago when Csaba was only seventeen. He had heard that there was to be a great wedding on an estate near Gran, a dozen miles from the village where he lived. There should be something for me there, said Csaba to himself, took his staff and set out along the dusty country roads.

"But he was out of luck. There was nothing at the wedding for him to steal. Should he go home empty-handed? At that moment he heard a great outcry from the guests assembled for the wedding feast — the young bride was dead! As the relatives and friends were already there, no lack of food and drink either, her burial was at once arranged for the following day. The wedding brought me no luck, thought Csaba, perhaps I shall fare better at the funeral, and he decided to stay.

"The next day Csaba took his place among the funeral guests to pay his respects to the deceased. The coffin lay with the lid open on a bier in the graveyard, where the guests filed past and took their leave. What a shock for Csaba! Aound the young bride's neck hung a priceless necklace. Csaba saw the necklace and thought: what good will that do her in the grave?

"He slept all day in a copse behind the graveyard and came back to the fresh grave late at night. No trouble for Csaba to lay his hands on pick and shovel, a bright moon shone down for him too, he dug down till he struck the coffin. Csaba broke it open: there she lay with her shimmering necklace. A pity to snap such a fine necklace, he thought, and putting his knee on her breast and his hands under her neck he jerked it upwards so that he could draw the necklace over her head.

"But what was this? A sigh escaped the girl's lips. The dead bride was still alive!"

"Csaba! That was you?"

An old Hungarian aristocrat, a former landowner, who had sat listening intently to the story, jumped to his feet excitedly.

"In 1908! That was the sensation of the year 1908!"

"Exactly as you say. But what had happened? At the wedding feast the bride had eaten fish, a bone had stuck in her throat, she had choked on the bone and died, or seemed to die. When Csaba gave that wrench to her neck he dislodged the bone in her throat and brought her back to life. As you say, the recovery of the bride caused a stir throughout the country, and not only in Hungary. But Csaba could not come forward to claim credit for his good deed, and so it was never known under what strange circumstances the bride had escaped from her grave and been restored to life."

The Hungarian landowner told us afterwards that as a result of this case a law was passed in Hungary requiring a medical examination and the issue of an official death certificate before a corpse could be buried. With his grave-yard escapade that moonlit night Csaba the thief had unknowingly changed the laws of his country.

Csaba's stories helped to relieve the terrible monotony of our evenings. Day in day out, from five in the afternoon until roll call the following morning, for fourteen of every twenty-four hours, we were locked into our room and waited for something to happen.

One of our few pastimes was chess. Everyone played chess. With charcoal we marked out boards on the tables where we ate and made primitive chess figures out of scraps of cloth or paper. Sexual frustration, feelings of hopelessness or simply boredom were sublimated into the sharp, narrow concentration of chess, allowing us briefly to forget. Chess tournaments channeled unattached passions and otherwise undirected violence and were arranged to last for months.

The only reading matter with which we were supplied was the Bible. Strangely enough, the classic texts of Marx and Engels were not allowed, but for the first few years, at least, there was never any shortage of Bibles. On the initiative of Dr. Hoppe, a former professor of philosophy from Leipzig who had been responsible for the censorship of Slovakian newspapers during the war, we started up a Bible study group that met regularly for over a year. Hoppe also arranged discussions on politics, philosophy, literature and other subjects. Men like Hoppe, who entered their lean prison years with a large fund of knowledge on which to draw, could escape into an introspection that was neutral and therefore not painful, and they were accordingly less susceptible than others to the debilitation of prison life. I learned that personal reminiscence alone was not enough to nourish one's mind, for the emergence from past into present was always deeply discouraging.

But Hoppe's natural curiosity battened on even these unpromising surroundings and gleaned matter for our edification. Thus throughout his stay in prison Hoppe sought his texts in an article that was submitted every evening to our scrutiny whether we wanted to take notice of it or not: the soles of our fellow prisoners' feet.

To the best of my knowledge, Hoppe was the first man to have hit on the idea of applying the techniques of palmistry to an analogous study of the feet. Hoppe owed his discovery to tiresome regulations concerning prisoners' sleep — the lights had to remain on throughout the night and we were required to lie on our back with our hands clasped behind the head. For anyone lying, like Hoppe, on a pallet on one of the long sides of the room, this regulation sleep posture meant that much of the field of vision would unwholesomely be taken up with the feet of the men lying opposite.

Hoppe, the man of science, did not make predictions. He confined himself to observations of the character of a man as it emerged here and now from the soles of his feet. To anyone who was interested Hoppe willingly discoursed on the characteristics he had learned to associate with flat or rounded heels, the curved grooves and wadded flesh wrinkles in the hollow of the foot, the degree of concavity of the hollow, the skin pad where the flesh bunched in anticipation of the toes, the splay of the toes: in short, with the foot in its entirety. He spoke confidently of meek or dominant toes, the podgy, retracted toe and the salient, ambitious toe, the sensitive and the brutal heel, the trustworthy and the untrustworthy, the good and the bad feet.

For a while Hoppe's foot lore became a fashion in Leopoldov. The theory seemed plausible enough, but it suffered from two obvious limitations. By definition it was the study exclusively of criminal feet; and its validity was more seriously impaired by the fact that our opinion of someone's character was already prejudiced by information acquired from sources other than his feet. Sixty men living together in one room very soon got to know one another. The demand for clinically virgin feet, on which to test the theory, had bizarre consequences. During the Hoppe period our natural interest in a new arrival immediately gravitated to his feet. By prior agreement we did not talk to new arrivals; we waited conspiratorially for the moment of the removal of boots and the revelation of feet. For a man who had only just arrived and who had been ostentatiously shunned by his fellow prisoners this attention suddenly fastened on the unbooting of his feet was extremely disconcerting.

All of us saw what Hoppe saw, but while he arrived at a confident diagnosis we merely ventured guesses. The Hoppe theory failed the test of all scientific hypotheses, the repeatability of an experiment with identical results, and eventually fell into decline.

While still under the influence of this theory, however,

I made the acquaintance of many inmates of Leopoldov that originated from an interest in their feet. Thus a pair of "incontinent and unruly feet" (Hoppe) provided me with a reliable letter of introduction to the character of Julius Thonet; two mute, blockish and corpselike feet paved the way for me into the sepulchral history of Slavo Zachar.

On the wall above Slavo Zachar's pallet hung the motto *He shall be released through death,* under which he had already slept for ten years. He was still only thirty-two. Until the age of twenty-two he had been an innkeeper in east Slovakia. Twice a week the purchase of supplies for his business took him into the local town. His business went quite well and for a couple of years he had been happily married. One day he hitched up horse and cart as usual and drove into town. He was halfway there when he found that he had forgotten his purse. Slavo Zachar turned the horse around and drove back home. The house appeared to be empty. He went upstairs to fetch the purse from under the mattress and found his wife naked in bed with the local horse dealer. Slavo Zachar rushed downstairs into the kitchen, grabbed a knife and ran back up to the bedroom before the lovers had recovered from their shock. He stabbed them both, hacked off the man's genitals and stuffed them into his wife's mouth until she had suffocated and the man bled to death. As soon as they were both dead he ran out of the house with the knife in his hand and gave himself up to the local police. He was arrested, tried and sentenced to life imprisonment in Leopoldov.

Slavo Zachar hardly ever spoke. His hair had turned gray and he already had the face of an old man. Other prisoners had told me of his case, but it was not until I had been in Leopoldov for some time that I heard his story from his own lips. Even ten years after, the telling of the story made him extremely agitated.

"You went berserk," I said. "But what do you feel now? Don't you regret it now?"

"Regret? I regret nothing."

After a pause he added, "I regret only that they did not die an even more terrible death."

This unexpected admission shocked me almost more than his account of the deed itself. Slavo Zachar was an ardent Bible reader who regularly assisted at mass in the prison chapel, but this one brief glimpse he gave me into his soul showed me a man sustained only by the passion of vengeance. This passion lit him, the energy it burned kept him alive, but the fanatic religiosity in which it burned gradually charred into a form of madness.

After twelve or fifteen years most men collapsed into living ruins like Slavo Zachar. The longest inhabitant of whom I knew was a murderer who had been sentenced to life imprisonment in 1902, pardoned in 1920 and again convicted of murder two years later. By the time I arrived in Leopoldov in 1948 this man had spent forty-six years of his life in prison — but one could not call it life, for the human being had long since been reduced to a torpid vegetable mass, the mere existence of flesh and bones. The only thing to elicit stirrings of life in this creature was a change in the routine to which he was accustomed. When a roll call was carried out on the left side instead of the right side of the yard, for example, requiring him to stand in a place different from the one to which he was used, he became pitifully disoriented, blundering around like a blind animal until someone led him back into line.

Not one of the long-term criminal offenders with whom I spoke expressed the slightest remorse for what he had done. Quite a number of them, like Slavo Zachar, had been sentenced for crimes involving a woman. Deprived of women, many prisoners resorted to grotesque means just to catch sight of a woman.

An ugly old spinster, for example, who regularly came to Leopoldov to give religious instruction, must have been gratified by the remarkably high attendance of her classes. I went along a couple of times myself, just to escape the Sunday boredom of our cell. The zealous old hag fished cardboard cutouts out of her satchel and pinned them venomously to the wall. The cardboard figures, miserably executed, represented the protagonists of the Bible story; Adam and Eve, the fall, the expulsion from the garden of Eden, and so on. I was so disgusted by the insipidity of these classes that I soon preferred the dreariness of my cell, but many prisoners were not deterred either by the foolishness or the repulsive appearance of the ancient missionary — despite everything she still managed to be a woman. She was impervious to the greedy anticipation that leered out of the faces of her regular Sunday crowd; thieves and murderers who sat nudging each other and smacking their lips were even awarded stars for consistent attendance. Quite possibly her attendance lists later reappeared in some erroneous statistic as evidence of the marked religiosity of long-term criminal offenders. From 1950 on, however, when the Communists began to do away with all vestiges of religion, the visits of the spinster missionary were brought to an end.

For all of us, criminals or politicals, the day-to-day problems of survival and, more importantly, the maintaining of a longer perspective, a glimmer of hope, were the same. Here I came to distinguish three groups.

The first group consisted of family men like myself. We were sustained by the belief, or hope, that some day we would be reunited with our families. On the whole, men who had families survived long prison sentences rather better than those who had not. Experience taught me that men between the ages of forty and fifty, in particular, showed a higher resistance to mental and physical strain than any other age group. Men of my age were in the prime of life; more, they were in the prime of family life, and from this they derived their stamina.

The second group was made up of men who held religious convictions. In a conservative, agrarian country like Slovakia religion played an important part in the national life, and this was reflected in the relatively high percentage of prisoners who were spiritually anchored in a religious belief. Belief helped, of that there was no doubt. This applied equally to the prison warders, whom I came to regard as also a kind of prisoner. I heard it said that the warder who led Tiso out onto the scaffold kissed his hand, asked his forgiveness and prayed for his soul.

The last group were those who had nothing, neither family nor belief, religious or otherwise. There were quite a lot of young men in this category. Once they lost hope they began to deteriorate very quickly. They seemed to be more prone to illness. Some of these young Slovaks had been students in Vienna, whom the Americans irresponsibly persuaded to cross the Slovakian border on espionage missions. If caught they were usually executed. The less fortunate ones were sent to Leopoldov for life. It was difficult to die in Leopoldov, even of natural causes. We were fed badly, but enough to survive. The prison hospital was abysmally equipped, but it tended the sick. Cases of tuberculosis were isolated in a separate wing. There were no razors; we were shaved by the prison barbers. For six years I ate only with a spoon. A very resolute man could hang himself from the bend in the heating pipe in the corner of the cells, but this was a difficult feat that no man I knew personally had accomplished.

For better or worse we were there to live. Perhaps I was among the lucky ones, for I had a reason to want to continue to live, I had hopes — had I not? — that those who had imprisoned me would keep faith and send me home when I had served my time. But meanwhile the days and the days and the days, ah! the buried years in Leopoldov that nothing would ever bring back.

In the Labyrinth

IN the autumn of 1948, not long after I had been committed to Leopoldov, President Benes died. He had abdicated only three months previously, a defeated man, making way for his Communist successor and former prime minister, Klement Gottwald. Within the space of little more than three years my personal fate had thus been closely allied to the political fortunes of three different presidents: indicted under Benes for offenses committed while Tiso was in power, I had been convicted and sent to prison in the name of President Gottwald. When the mid-century succession of the Communist Gottwald followed on the heels of the Democrat Benes I was forty-six years old. I was almost as old as my century. I had grown with it, I had warped with it. Sentenced during the first half of it, I would serve most of that sentence during the second; and in a manner of speaking my century would serve it with me.

The more the country's social and political system came to resemble a prison, the more accurately the prison within that prison reflected society outside. Almost overnight the country found itself surrounded by walls. Inside those walls, as inside the fortress of Leopoldov, a generation of political turbulence was immured. Czechoslovakia's past spoke a babble of four languages, comporting itself now nationalist and separatist, now fascist, now anti-clerical and anti-fascist, now democratic, now Communist — all these factions, doused but not extinguished, smoldered on in Leopoldov too.

The most recent of these factions, the Communists, showed early on their particular aptitude for building walls, as befitted the new architects of the state. For some time it remained unclear what kind of structure they had in mind, or according to what plan it would be built. First they circumscribed the site, like a medieval town, with a protective wall that both enclosed and shut out. This monumental task was achieved in about the same time that it took to have me extradited, impounded and tried, and it could be argued that among the materials with which it was accomplished some had been quarried from the rubble of my past. My trial, the trials of the aggressors, criminals and collaborators, were not merely concurrent with the walling in of the country in which they took place; they helped to furnish the blocks and mortar with which those walls were built. The future was being incarcerated in our past.

When the bulwark between East and West was complete the Communists initiated a building program within the country itself. According to sources whose information became available in Leopoldov not long after the event, the foundations of this program were laid at a meeting of the Central Committee of the Czechoslovakian Communist Party in June 1948. The general secretary, Rudolf Slansky, submitted his report on a session of the Cominform and a resolution it had passed concerning the Communist Party of Yugoslavia. The resolution declared that the only reliable indicator of loyalty to the cause of socialism was loyalty to the Soviet Union itself. It condemned as "bourgeois nationalism" all strategic routes to the socialist goal that deviated from the course prescribed by the Soviet Union.

The Central Committee endorsed the Cominform resolution with criticism of similar deviationists it had detected in its own ranks, notably the bourgeois nationalists among the Slovakian Communists. They were not named at the time, but the foundations thus laid were broad enough to accommodate any conceivable future requirement. Meanwhile the People's Courts were mysteriously transforming themselves into tribunals disguised as State Courts, and an authority not apparently connected with either of these began to practice its own form of justice by dispensing with the process of trial altogether. During 1948 and 1949 outhouses on the perimeters of that vast, still indeterminate Communist edifice that had yet to be built sprang up all over the country, notably in the vicinity of uranium mines. There were regular human consignments from Leopoldov to Joachimstal, few of which returned; radiation, apparently, was injurious to their health. But the few who did come back from the mines and who had sampled the accommodation of the outhouses positively identified them as labor camps under the administration of the Security Service. The workers in these camps were all prisoners on loan, some from institutions like Leopoldov, others who had been transferred without benefit of trial from a very much larger penal settlement whose area coincided with that of Czechoslovakia.

Much of the year 1949 was taken up with such preparatory measures; drainage and leveling of the land. In September of that year expatriate Hungarians living in Bratislava reported to their countrymen in Leopoldov that the Communists had staged a trial against Laszlo Rajk and fellow conspirators in Budapest. Rajk, Szönyi and Szalai were found guilty of having formed an organization to overthrow the state and sentenced to death. Only three months later Traitscho Kostoff was condemned to death after a similar political trial in Bulgaria, but the real thrust of these trials appeared to be directed less at Hungary or Bulgaria than Yugoslavia and the subversive example of Tito. In Leopoldov it was rumored that the Communists in Prague had approached the party leadership in Moscow with a request for security advisers to be sent. These sinister rumors were confirmed in October by the arrival of Makarov and Likhachov, who had managed the Rajk trial in Budapest. It was said that a second delegation of security advisers, headed by Boyarsky, had followed not long after; responsible solely to the Soviet Ministry of State Security, at that time controlled by Beria, they wielded extraordinary powers. We felt the impact of those powers ourselves. A sudden inrush of summarily convicted men from the district court prison filled the cells in Leopoldov and overflowed into the corridors. The new arrivals reported that throughout November mass arrests had been taking place. Cells were urgently required in the district court prison to accommodate the thousands of Czech Socialists, Catholics, and Social Democrats who were being arrested. They were accused of belonging to an underground conspiracy that had maintained connections with imperialist intelligence services and anti-Communist organizations abroad. The cliques of high-caliber political prisoners in Leopoldov who analyzed these events during the long winter evenings were puzzled at first by the lack of a discernible pattern in the new wave of arrests. It was learned that a witness by the name of Kopecky or Borszeky, who was to give evidence at the forthcoming political trials in Czechoslovakia, had already played a part in the Laszlo Rajk trial in Budapest. Was this a coincidence, or was it a deliberate attempt to establish a connection between the trials in the one country and in the other with the aim of reinforcing Communist claims of an international conspiracy? Was there a need to look for any pattern at all in the apparently random selection of political victims, other than the guiding, misguiding hand of Moscow? The arbitrary procedure of the Soviet advisers installed in Prague might be explained by their unfamiliarity with the intricacies of Czechoslovakian politics. Czech prosecutors would have included some prominent names absent from the Makarov/Boyarsky list and omitted a number of others. Where were the fifth columnists in the party's own ranks, the deviationists, the Slovakian separatists and bourgeois nationalists for whom the Cominform and the Central Committee had been digging in June of the previous year? Was their turn still to come? And how many more were to come? These questions were left hanging in the air, stunned by the paradox that although, at last, it was now possible to recognize that mysterious artifact which had begun to rise on the master builders' foundations, no one was any the wiser as to what it was for. And here came the final parallel between the society outside Leopoldov and the society inside, in which one could spend a long time, a lifetime perhaps, for lifetimes were now short, without discovering how the whole was made up of its parts, what lay behind the next wall or where the next corridor led. Czechoslovakia, too, had been turned into a labyrinth.

A few months before the Rajk trial in Budapest I was assigned with the Hungarian thieves Csaba and Boros to a building project in one of the back courts of Leopoldov, which the prison administration had decided to have repaved. While Benes was being lowered into a freshly dug grave, old paving stones were being trundled out of the fortress gates to a local builder's yard and pulverized to a moldy dust as an admixture for low-grade concrete. When the old paving had been removed from the back court we began to cart cobblestones from a huge pile lying outside the fortress walls. After several weeks, when half the court had already been paved, the heap of cobblestones that some joker had ordered had not noticeably diminished — there would have been enough to pave the entire fortress. The prisoners chuckled over this outsize prank that had been played on the prison authorities, but they had a different word for it: sabotage. Who had ordered the cobblestones? The project foreman was held responsible and spent a blind week in the dark cell on half rations, but the miscreant was never found out. The unused cobblestones remained lying outside the fortress for years.

In the grassy wilderness surrounding the newly cobbled court — once a nuns' garden, it was said — the prison works committee decided to set up a pig farm. It was an ambitious project, with a planned capacity of several hundred pigs, which meant that a lot of pigpens had to be built. The bricklayers assigned to this task were thirty Catholic priests and a couple of bishops. On the strength of my knowledge of business management and my experience as a supplier of building materials the works committee regarded me as sufficiently qualified to supervise the construction of a pig farm. Accordingly I was appointed as the overseer of the ecclesiastic bricklayers.

My bricklayers were not in fact required to lay bricks but merely to assemble blocks of an unidentifiable, porous material in the form of loosely mortared, rudimentary walls. They did not have to be tall, solid, or even particularly straight walls — the only requirement was that they did not immediately fall down. Despite these lenient standards the building of the pigpens made little progress. The spiritual masons of the church were very incompetent bricklayers, were wholly unqualified to do any manual work at all. They made efforts, but they tired easily, their hands were soft, their feet liturgically slow. I applied to the works committee for reinforcements, but they maliciously encumbered me with help by sending thieves, murderers and vocational atheists to argue with the priests for a day or two.

Every morning I was given the norms to be fulfilled that day, so many yards of wall per man, every evening I had to report that again the norms had not been met. Norms were generally not met, for in most cases they could easily be fiddled, but it was not possible to overlook yards of unbuilt wall. I exhorted the clerics' secular powers by appealing to their better, spiritual half. The entire population of Leopoldov was watching their work, I said. Would they allow the reputation of their church to be tarnished by bungling an order for a pigsty? No less was at stake. The clerics agreed that that would indeed be a sorry state of affairs, and for a while there was a slight improvement. The works committee responded by raising the norms. The priests capitulated. Their rations were cut by a third, their Church foundered, and threatened to capsize in the quagmire of Leopoldov's pigsties.

On reduced rations myself, I no longer attempted to meet the norms but merely to keep myself and my bricklayers fit enough to put in a day's work. And here, quite unexpectedly, it was their very incompetence that came to our aid. Impatient with the slow progress that was being made, the works committee decided not to wait for the project to be completed but to start installing pigs in the pens that had already been built. Several dozen suckling pigs duly arrived and were quartered in their priest-built enclosures. More priests were seconded as pig minders, and the work site in the prison yard soon began to resemble scenes from a grotesque Nativity in which swine had supplanted ox and ass. Perhaps it was Ota Obuch, irreverently embroidering the doctrine of transubstantiation, who put the much more practical idea into my head that fodder for suckling pigs could equally be used as nourishment for priests.

The piglets received a generous allowance of skimmed milk, delivered to the prison each morning. Not much bigger than a man's forearm when they were first brought to us, the piglets evidently thrived on this diet. In a very short time they had doubled their size and sported pink, enviably healthy snouts. The idea of passing the cut in our rations on to the pigs by discreetly purloining a bucket or two of their milk would have occurred to any hungry man much sooner had the milk looked a little more appetizing — a greenish liquid under transparent, floating layers of scum. However, when I examined the encrusted vats more closely, dredging the bottom with a ladle gently so as not to disturb the scum, I found a firm, wholesome sediment with a quite acceptable taste. It seemed that all my problems with the bricklayer-priests would thus be solved.

Every day a vat of skimmed milk unobtrusively made its way to the foreman's hut, where I sat with my accountant's ledger and charts, supervising the progress of the pig farm project. At half-hour intervals, according to a rota system that the priests arranged among themselves, famished clerics came one after another to consult me on some aspect of the building schedule. My advice was administered in beakers, which the visitors invariably quaffed in one draft. What I had to communicate was received with greedy reverence, like a long-awaited sacrament. When the subject had been exhausted there was never any need for questions; only for a moment's contemplation of the matter that had been ingested.

The works committee was impressed. Suspicious at first of the new consultation system I had introduced, critical of wasted time, they were fully persuaded by the results. Productivity rose. Pens were punctually completed, porkers installed. And most important of all: the clandestine transfer of energy from pig to priest had been effected without detriment to the former while clearly benefiting the latter. After only two weeks, however, the skimmed milk honeymoon abruptly came to an end — because of the priests' greed.

One morning a delegation of priests arrived at my hut with a request for a second vat of milk to be placed at their colleagues' disposal. I said that a second vat was out of the question. One vat could be managed, at a pinch, but two would definitely be missed, and then nobody would get anything. The delegation wagged its head and went away, but returned ten minutes later to negotiate a compromise. They agreed that appropriating a second vat would entail too high a risk. What about one and a half? The milk could be discreetly drawn off from all the vats, one at a time, and conveyed to my hut in a separate container. I rejected the plan: it would attract too much attention. I asked if the priests were dissatisfied with what they were getting. The delegation explained that they were having difficulties arranging a rota system to divide twenty beakers of milk per day equitably among thirty-two contenders. They were all entitled to milk at least every other day, and some of them received milk on consecutive days. This was where the trouble lay. Who should be the consecutive drinkers? They were all agreed that the simplest solution would not be a better division but a division of more — a beaker per man per day. I remained adamant. The ensuing squabbles over this point became so heated that in disgust I applied to the works committee for a transfer, and for the remaining weeks the pig farm project lasted the priests got no skimmed milk at all.

I was not particularly surprised by this disgraceful episode. I had shared a common cell with the priests during the couple of months we worked together, and had thus become familiar with the workings of the priestly mind. They lacked all sense of comradeship. Perhaps it would be fairer to say: comradeship toward their own kind. Celibate in their personal and solitary in their professional lives, the priests had never learned the rudiments of companionship naturally acquired in the relationships with family and colleagues. The man could not be detached from the office: he was his office. And he was qualified for this office firstly by the provision of material things — vestments, ritual, a congregation and a place of worship. Deprived of these things he ceased to be a priest, but without reverting to being just a normal man. He became a priestly man.

Fifty or sixty priestly men confined in one place were like prima donnas sharing a dressing room. The cell buzzed and hummed with the arias of prayer, each claiming the individual attention of a common God. The opera of the church, as enacted in Leopoldov, suffered from too many soloists and the absence of a chorus.

Outside his prayers the subjects that most occupied the priestly mind were food and housekeepers. Here his training stood him in good stead. The lively fantasy of the theologian, accustomed to range with ease between the ramparts of heaven and the fires of hell, substantiating space, had no trouble at all in conjuring a side of ham or a larded goose. Liver pies bodied forth from frayed cuffs, baked apples were plucked from fingertips. The priests dined on their imagination. The delicacies they ordered were cooked and served by equally immaterial housekeepers. It was not until after dinner, when their masters were gorged and snoozed and fresh for bed, that those housekeepers were summoned from pantries of the imagination into bodily presence between the sheets.

I had always taken for granted that the natural effect of enforcing celibacy on priests was to enforce priests on their housekeepers, but I was taken aback by the candor, at times the blasphemy, with which they discussed the subject among themselves. In the cell in Leopoldov I heard it suggested that the relationship between priest and housekeeper was a mirror image of that between Joseph and Mary; on the one side conception, which doctrine required to be agamogenetic, on the other side no question of asexuality so long as there was no conception. Most of the priests had sexual relationships with their housekeepers. They regarded it as an adjunct of holy office, a fringe benefit, like tithes and a free house.

During my first and second year in Leopoldov the priests were still allowed a measure of religious freedom. They had breviaries and Bibles; from time to time they could celebrate mass in the prison chapel. But from about the spring of 1950, when the trials of church dignitaries began, Bibles were confiscated and the celebration of mass banned. The priests responded to the prohibition with conspiratorial relish. Illegality lifted morale. Among lay prisoners confidence in the religious order was restored; the pig farm travesty was forgotten. Slovakian warders smuggled the host into one hand of the priesthood and received absolution from the other. When the Slovak was replaced by an anti-clerical Czech administration the flow of contraband wine was docked. Heroism infused piety. Several fathers distinguished themselves as adroit organizers of the raisins from which the communion wine now had to be pressed. Spoons served as chalices, crumbs of black bread were transfigured into the host.

Over a hundred clerics languished in Leopoldov at this time. To the best of my knowledge there was not a single Protestant among them. Some of them had openly criticized the government and received long sentences for conspiring against the state, but many were imprisoned simply because they were priests. When Christmas came around, half a dozen would be amnestied and sent home as evidence of the Communists' lenient policy toward the church. The rest of us listened, in deepening gloom, to an endless recording of "Silent Night," piped over loudspeakers into the corridors, and attended the prison orchestra's annual performance of *Fidelio*.

After weeks in the undiluted company of priests I was glad to be restored to the lay friendships I had formed in my first cell. Several familiar faces had gone. For Csaba, seasonally imprisoned, the gates of Leopoldov opened with the coming of spring. He returned to his bawdy daughters and the pursuit of poultry. Welser, the snoring grocer, had gone home to the decorous bosom of his wife and the pursuit of vegetables, from which history had unkindly separated him. But there were plenty of other acquaintances that could be resumed where they had been left off; in particular the more thorough acquaintance of Julius Thonet, whose reckless nature had been predicted by Hoppe from a perusal of the soles of his feet.

Thonet was in a shocking physical state. Since our last

meeting he had grown very thin, his body was covered with bruises, and he had lost the tip of his nose.

For a brief spell he had apparently worked on an assignment with a gypsy. Thonet, who was unable to open his mouth without making a careless remark, had said something that offended the gypsy. He felt his honor insulted and demanded an apology. Thonet refused. On parade the next morning the coal-eyed gypsy had whisked a blade out of his pocket and sliced off the tip of Thonet's nose. The gypsy was clapped in irons and sentenced to two weeks in the fortress dungeons, but his punishment couldn't restore Thonet's nose.

"Perhaps it'll teach him a lesson," said Obuch, another victim of Thonet's many indiscretions. "Less nose to poke into other people's business."

The reason for Thonet's bruised body and loss of weight was even more bizarre than his loss of nose. He was an insatiable tobacco addict. He smoked away his meager prison wage and when that was gone began to smoke away his food by bartering it for cigarettes. And still Thonet could not get enough. He pleaded, cadged, lied and stole. All this made him very unpopular. Occasionally it led to blows. Thonet must have observed that some of his fellow prisoners took pleasure in giving him a beating; they actually felt better afterwards. He offered them a preposterous deal: free beatings in exchange for cigarettes. Terms were negotiated, the number of blows per cigarette. Thonet paid in pain. A length of hemp was procured from the prison stores, immersed in water, knotted, dried. Thonet supervised the manufacture of his torture instrument personally. Whenever he ran out of tobacco he voluntarily underwent a whipping.

Some of us tried to put a stop to this degrading spectacle.

Thonet insisted on his rights: it was a private arrangement between two consenting parties. We argued that anything we were forced to witness was equally of concern to us, and we had not given our consent. Some shared our view, others supported Thonet. Hoppe agreed to chair a debate on condition that a majority vote would be accepted by those who thought differently. The vote went in Thonet's favor, not because a majority wanted to see free will upheld, but because they wanted to see Thonet beaten.

The man who allowed himself to be flogged in exchange for cigarettes was the scion of a very wealthy family. The Thonet brothers were the sole heirs of an international furniture concern. Julius had led a leisurely, aristocratic life with more than enough of everything, including tobacco, on his estate in central Slovakia. At some time in the late 1930s he tired of his wife and divorced her — a private arrangement, as Thonet would say, which would not have concerned anyone else had his wife not happened to be a Jewess. She vanished without trace, whether abroad or into a mass grave could not later be established. Thonet, either very foolish or politically very naive, stayed on at his estate playing billiards while Russian tanks advanced and his countrymen fled across the border. When the war was over he was arrested and put on trial on a charge of racial discrimination. He was accused of having divorced a Jewish wife at a time when to do so had meant a serious risk to her life. Thonet sneeringly told the judges that if they thought Hitler had been in the bedroom when he quarreled with his wife then they were asses. He was not a ventriloquist's dummy. He was sorry about what had happened to the Jews, not sorry that he had divorced his wife. The one had nothing to do with the other. The court saw the matter differently, however, and sentenced him to ten years.

After divorcing his Jewish wife Thonet had married his

Aryan housekeeper. Outside prison she continued to care for her erratic husband throughout his years in Leopoldov, visiting him regularly every two months with food parcels that Thonet converted into tobacco before she was out of the prison gates. For the next few days, at least, no beatings took place. Hoppe, shrewd reader of men's soles, took the view that it was not addiction that made Thonet submit to the humiliation of these beatings but a guilty conscience on account of the divorced Jewish wife.

For some months Thonet and I worked together in Leopoldov's furniture factory. The heir of an international furniture concern hardly knew one end of a saw from another, but it turned out that we would only be entrusted with the lowest-grade work of polishing, so there was little scope for him to do any serious damage. The factory manufactured a couple of hundred cupboards per month, all of which had to be polished. It was monotonous work and it made one dizzy, because one breathed in the fumes of the methylated spirits mixed with the polish. Like most unpleasant work it was reserved for intellectuals, politicals and priests. Two men worked at each bench. I polished one half of a cupboard, Thonet the other.

Among the polishers there was a Slovak schoolteacher, a huge man, as broad as a barn door. We noticed that by about two or three in the afternoon this fellow had always got through his share of polish. Occasionally he went up to the overseer to ask for more, but for some reason he usually preferred to take his bowl around and get a refill from the rest of us.

Thonet's curiosity soon got the better of him, and the next time the schoolteacher sidled over to our bench Thonet sternly asked him how on earth he managed to get through so much polish so quickly. A little shamefaced, the schoolteacher replied that it was a disgrace, he knew it, but there it was, from time to time he couldn't control himself — he drank it. Thonet roared with laughter, clapped him on the shoulder, and handed him his can. The schoolteacher drained it on the spot.

In this phenomenal quaffer of polish Thonet had undoubtedly met his match. He had been imbibing it daily for the past three months. We told him he was drinking poison, and that it was just a matter of time before it would kill him. The schoolteacher ignored our warnings. From week to week we watched his face become grayer. His body wasted away; the skin hung loosely from his bones. And one morning he keeled over with a great crash, clutched his groin and rolled back his eyes. Four men carried him to the infirmary on the door of the cupboard he had been polishing, but he was dead before they got him outside.

Not long after the death of the schoolteacher Thonet had himself transferred to another assignment. One of his cronies was starting up a chicken farm. Thonet asked me to join him. The job had one obvious advantage: there would be plenty of eggs to eat. It was a tempting offer, but for some reason I turned it down. Perhaps I was wary of Thonet, or perhaps I had had enough of farm projects already. Chicken minding was certainly more attractive than door polishing, and I might have accepted if I had not been offered a job as accountant in the furniture factory at about the same time that Thonet's chicken farm project came up.

Until about 1949 the furniture factory had been run as a private enterprise by an ingenious businessman called Quitt. He had been granted a license by the prison authorities to manufacture a given number of cupboards, using cheap convict labor and a handful of specialist craftsmen whom he was allowed to import from outside. Working relations between civilians and convicts did not run into any of the expected difficulties, Quitt made money, convicts were kept busy, and for a long time the prison administration was content with the arrangement.

All this changed when the Communists came to power. Their business expropriation program sounded the knell for capitalist entrepreneurs all over the country, including Quitt and his manufacture of cupboards inside the walls of Leopoldov. Quitt managed to hang on to his business much longer than most, probably because of a discreet ownership clause in his contract with the prison administration that the expropriators overlooked. They got onto Quitt too, however, at about the time I started polishing his cupboard doors.

Promoted from polishing to accounting, I soon discovered that a certain amount of polishing would also be required of me in my new employment: a discreet polishing of accounts. My first task was to take inventory of the assets of Quitt Cupboards Ltd. After two days' stocktaking I drew up a scrupulous list and presented it to my employer, who promptly tore it up and tossed it into the wastepaper basket.

"That's your list, not mine," he said, looking at me sternly. "Come along with me."

I followed him into the warehouse.

"How much plywood d'you suppose we've got in here?"

"Approximately two hundred square yards," I said. "I've measured it out."

"Then you've measured badly. I always measure by eye, and my eye is infallible. I tell you, there's not an inch more than eighty square yards of plywood in here."

"Eighty? That's ridiculous."

"Eighty is what I said. So write it down."

Quitt's eye and my measurements continued to reach very different conclusions with regard to the amounts of hardwood, glue, scrolls of varnish paper and screws that were stocked on the premises, and the list that was duly submitted to the state inspectors served more as an index of Quitt's foresight than as an inventory of his worldly goods. Expropriated without compensation but not yet ousted, he was retained in what now became a state enterprise in a commissary function, fulfilling the improbable production norms demanded by his new masters despite the fact that the supply of raw materials consistently fell short. Quitt kept up this remarkable balancing act for several years before he was found out, and then only because someone had denounced him. Like hundreds of other businessmen in similar positions, he was charged with sabotage and sentenced to a long term of imprisonment.

The conviction of capitalist saboteurs fueled Communist propaganda, but if the working classes upheld convictions in one sense they did not share them in another. They found their hourly wage rate suddenly cut from fourteen to eleven crowns: the new economic policy required a breathing space after the debilitation of free enterprise. Several thousand workers at the Coburg plant near Bratislava, in agreement with a breathing space, perhaps, but not at the cost of their own economic strangulation, expressed their point of view by going on strike. Six months later the leaders of the strike were enjoying the benefits of free accommodation in another state-owned enterprise, Leopoldov. In effect they had been sentenced for taking at face value the Communist claim that the workers were now running the country. There were many others who made the same mistake. For example the workers in timber and cellulose industries, who were foolish enough — on the assumption that one could not steal what one owned — to carry away from factory premises waste wood for fueling stoves at home. They were convicted of theft of state property nonetheless.

Reports of these encouraging developments in the world outside were smuggled into Leopoldov by the civilian go-betweens, who spent outside the prison walls the money they earned inside. Their outside information, pieced together with the inside information to which I had access in my capacity as Quitt's accountant, brought to light an interesting economic record.

I knew that production costs for a given piece of furniture, for example, including wages and materials, amounted to a hundred crowns. I also knew that the furniture *Kombinat* (so called since Quitt's demise), which placed the orders and paid the bills, sold the same piece of furniture to state-owned furniture stores for two hundred crowns. From my civilian colleagues I learned that the furniture stores charged five hundred crowns for the identical article, and for those who took advantage of generous state loans to furnish their houses in weekly installments the final price would be closer to seven hundred. Party officials paid the factory price, as a matter of course.

I was glad of the contact with the civilian workers at the furniture factory, as it kept me in touch with the ordinary affairs of ordinary people. Although I had permission to see visitors once every couple of months there were no members of my own family still in Czechoslovakia who could have come to see me, and even for my wife's relatives it was a long journey.

Usually it was Helga, my wife's eldest sister, who sat on the far side of the screen whenever I was led into the visitors' room. She stood up and kissed me through the grid. How was she? Fine. And how was Ladislav? He was fine too. She talked about their day-to-day life in Pressburg, which she obstinately refused to call Bratislava. Three visits took place at the same time, a warder sitting behind each prisoner's chair, so we had to be careful what we said. I asked her about my own family, and would give her a significant look, reminding her to answer the question in what was referred to as the Bubb code. Helga said it had been unusually cold in Geneva. The youngest child was three years old and would probably have learned to skate before he first saw his father. Helga had to bite her lip whenever she spoke of my youngest son.

"Ten minutes!" The warder behind me stood up. Already it was time for her to go. She never knew it, but if I hurried I would be able to catch a last, unauthorized glimpse of her before she left. The corridor off the visitors' room led directly to the furniture factory, and in the factory there was a whitewashed window, with a peephole where the paint had been scratched off in one corner, which looked down into the prison visitors' waiting room. After Helga's visits I always sprinted to this window to see her, however briefly, once more. Why did I do this? It was a sight I could hardly bear. In the waiting room, alone, comforted by her handkerchief, she gave vent to the tears she denied herself in my presence.

Three sprints to the whitewashed window, three times the sight of my sister-in-law confiding in her handkerchief: six months had passed. This was how I measured and how I was to remember my time in Leopoldov, bartering minutes for months, recording the years of my prime in half a dozen miniatures. Three times Helga, six months polishing doors and polishing accounts, and then no second glimpses, because I was assigned to work in the surrounding fields where there was no window for the afterthought, and then no glimpses at all, because by the autumn of 1950 Helga was dead.

Only short-term criminal offenders were assigned to jobs outside the prison walls, so my inclusion in what was known as the "carrot commando" must have been due to some administrative oversight. Digging up carrots all day long was not easy work, but I would have done anything for a chance to get out. The view from outside of the place where one is imprisoned cannot be described as less than exhilarating. For a couple of weeks, until the mistake was discovered, I enjoyed that sense of exhilaration to the full.

The foreman on the job set a cracking pace, because he was paid a premium to do so. He worked at one end of a row of twenty or thirty men, who took their cue from him. If a man failed to keep up, his rations were cut, leading him into the notorious vicious circle that all prisoners feared. The soil was heavy, and I had to stand on the spade each time in order to get it down and loosen the plant. After four or five days of this I knew that I would soon not be able to keep up.

A pickpocket from Neutra, a slight boy aged about twenty, must have noticed I was in trouble, for on the way back from work one evening he fell in with me and opened, as at first it seemed to me, a strange conversation. Who was I working for, the pickpocket asked me. For nobody, I said. Nobody must be a hard master, replied the boy archly, putting his head on one side and squinting at me. I said nothing. After a while, when he had finished taking his sideways stock of me, the boy announced that he didn't think much of Nobody; he preferred to work for himself. He asked me if I thought he looked tired. No, I said to my own surprise, he looked amazingly fresh. Hello there, answered the boy with a low whistle, now how could that be? Wasn't I twice his size, twice as strong? Better to be one's own master than to work for Nobody, said the boy, shaking his head, and gave another of his queer whistles. Hadn't it occurred to me that one could keep up with the row but dig up only half as many carrots? One could do it if one stayed down the line, away from the foreman. Easy as pie. Don't dig for every carrot, don't even try to take it out, said the boy quickly, squinting both sides, leave it in the ground and just tear off the leaves. Every other carrot, just the leaves. Bundle together at the end of each row, lots of carrots, lots of leaves: did anybody ever count the leaves of a carrot, the leaves of *thirty* carrots? He pulled his pockets inside out for an answer. Nobody, I said. The boy laughed, and we parted inside the prison gates.

For the next ten days, thanks to my clever pickpocket companion, we had an easy time. Take one and miss one; carrot for carrot, leaf for leaf, we worked in a peaceful conspiracy at the far end of the line. Other flagging members were also let in on the secret. When the job of harvesting the carrots was done, and the foreman was taken aside to be paid his premium, we knew that about half the carrots were still out there in the field. Quite a few more, in cartridge-belt fashion, were tucked into our belts under our shirts and had already made their way back to Leopoldov.

On the last evening, on the road leading back to the prison, we came across an old man sitting in a cart whose horse was dying between the shafts. The horse had collapsed, snapping the harness, and lay in the road on its flank, with flared nostrils, making feeble burrowing movements with its hoofs. We stood around in silence, watching the dying animal.

"Seems to be digging his grave, swear he does," said the old man. He leaned over and spat into the dust.

"You lads get him onto this cart for me and bring us as far as the gates, you can eat him."

There was a murmur of approval from the crowd of men. One of them moved forward. The horse lashed out.

"Easy, easy."

We waited hungrily for the horse to die.

A few minutes later the horse groaned and shuddered. We could take him now, the old man said. We heaved the carcass up onto the cart and dragged it, the old man still perched on his seat, back to the prison gates and into the front court.

Cooks and butchers were summoned. Parts of the horse were marked for steak, other parts for stew. The old man shook our hands and left. Within a couple of hours his ancient nag had been cut up and cooked; an entire magazine of carrots, our last day's surreptitious harvest, went into the stew, and that evening I enjoyed the best meal I had eaten in more than three years. Even after the horse had been divided among the field workers, butchers and cooks, there was still a share for some of my cell companions — Oberle, Obuch, Boros and Thonet, all got a bowl of stew.

Long before he ate his stew, which gave us all diarrhea, Thonet's skin had begun to turn an alarming yellowish color. He cheerfully attributed it to his smoking. In the meantime, thanks to the chicken farm, he did at least get enough to eat: as many eggs as he liked. As often as I passed the chicken farm I would see Thonet and his fellow supervisor cracking eggs on their teeth and swallowing them whole. But despite the eggs, and despite the much less frequent beatings, from which egg trading had liberated him, there was something wrong with Thonet.

He became uncharacteristically docile, soft-mannered, sentimentally whimsical. In the courtyard beneath our cell two lime trees grew. One could see the tips of these trees through the window. Between the lime trees a wild rosebush flowered from early summer till September; the only greenery, apart from weeds and grass, to be seen inside the fortress walls. One had to climb up into the casement to see the rosebush. From about the time he began to turn yellow, Thonet would sit in this recess for hours, his unmistakable tipless nose in profile against the window. His thoughts wandered; sometimes he talked to himself. The lime trees and the rosebush reminded him of his former estate. Every day, walking around the courtyard with me, Thonet would stoop over his rosebush and touch a pale pink blossom with trembling hands. "Look at that! Look at that!" I walked him back and forth a few times until he had quieted down. Again he stopped by the rosebush. "Just look at that!" I reassured him I could see it very well, but it seemed that Thonet must have been looking at something else. There was something else he wanted to convey to me, which lay beyond the mere rosebush I saw in the courtyard. Throughout that summer he continued to suck eggs, his shaking hands beside the rosebush seemed to become even yellower, or perhaps it was a change in the roses themselves, deepening into a richer autumnal color. Why did none of us realize? What use was Hoppe's unruly lore if it failed to read a mortal sickness from the soles of a man's feet? The yellowing of Thonet and his business partner had set in from the initiation of their poultry farm. Within less than a year they were both dead. Of jaundice — and here the wayward Thonet would have laughed — caused by a surfeit of chickens' eggs.

The Nemesis of Boros

AFTER five years in prison, and still only halfway through his sentence, the handsome young Boros was getting increasingly unrestful. Another five years! In his sleep he no longer talked about the Warsaw ghetto; it seemed he had put that behind him. He began to talk about escape.

Escape from Leopoldov was not as difficult as some of the old hands liked to make it out to be. I could have made an escape while assigned to the carrot commando simply by running across the fields; and there would be other chances to come. The problem was not how to get over the prison walls, but what to do once you were outside them. I knew of nobody who had managed the much more difficult transition across the border between Czechoslovakia and the West. But Boros didn't want to go west. He wanted to escape back into the past, to the Hungary he had known before the war. He would disappear into the crowds of Budapest and resume his old profession. It never occurred to Boros that in fact he might not like the new Hungary, and that it would now be much more difficult for him to live the kind of life there he remembered. Out of touch with changing realities, Boros and his expatriate friends were as much the prisoners of their own imagination as they were of the Czechoslovakian state.

III

Who was I to warn Boros not to risk an escape? My own family, impoverished but secure, had already put down their roots in the West. Besides, I had a half-arse sentence: another three years and I would be home. Half-baked caution was all very well for prisoners sitting it out on half their arse, but for long-term offenders like Boros the prospects were different. Even more important than that: escape for Boros did not mean the mere removal of his body to the other side of Leopoldov's walls. After years of the drought of confinement his adventurous soul thirsted for a challenge.

Despite all my intentions not to jeopardize my good record by risking an abortive escape, I nearly succumbed to the stir of this challenge myself. An opportunity to escape presented itself at the time Boros and I were working on an assignment at the tileworks in Piestany, involving one of the most curious episodes in my prison life.

The Piestany tileworks were situated about fifty kilometers from Leopoldov. For several months a team of laborers, including Boros and myself, was driven to Piestany in the morning, spent the day working at the tile factory and returned to the prison at nightfall. The problem of getting over the prison walls was thus already solved for anyone intending to escape, even if there were no question of making a jump for it en route. The prison truck was netted, and we were escorted by two guards armed with machine guns, who sat facing each other at the rear end. A third guard sat in the front beside the driver. For some reason we were always required to sit in the same place. My seat was directly behind the driver. Boros sat beside one of the guards at the other end.

It was a pleasant trip out to Piestany, about an hour's drive. Most of us sat and enjoyed the countryside, but its merits were lost on would-be escapers like Boros, who were only looking for a break. And finally Boros got his break.

The incident occurred one rainy evening on the way back to Leopoldov. After work that day I had been called in for a word with the factory manager, and as a result of this delay I climbed up into the waiting truck almost ten minutes late. The men were tired; the guard told me not to bother to squeeze through to the front end of the truck but to take the vacant seat beside him. This order saved my life. About halfway to Leopoldov the truck skidded on the wet road, charged over an embankment and overturned. The men sitting in the back were thrown sideways into the enclosing net, which didn't break but gave way sufficiently to absorb most of the impact. There was terrible confusion inside the net. Trapped in the mesh, men began to panic, struggling wildly not to escape but just to get out of the crush of bodies. It must have been an hour before we were released. The two guards at the back, both unhurt, took stock of the damage. Their colleague up front in the driver's cab was concussed, the driver himself had a broken leg. Several of the prisoners had also broken limbs, and two of them were dead: the man occupying my regular seat behind the driver had broken his neck. I escaped with bruises. The guards counted heads, dead and alive, and a very shaken band of men was driven back to the prison in another truck. Such was the confusion that it was not until our arrival in Leopoldov, long after nightfall, that the guards noticed their mistake. One man was missing: Boros.

A posse of warders searched the accident site early the next morning, hoping to find Boros, dead or alive, lying somewhere under a bush. No sign of Boros anywhere. They even waded through a nearby river, armed with poles, and sounded the surrounding marshland. He was not there either. Boros had vanished.

Only three days after Boros got his break those of us

who were not hospitalized found ourselves back at work in Piestany again. I had been made foreman on the job because of my experience running my own tileworks in Deutsch-Proben. The Deutsch-Proben factory was about half the size, but with three times the production capacity of the plant in Piestany, and much of my time there as shop-floor foreman was spent with the object of depressing production still further. My reasons for doing this were not merely malicious. Slow, inefficient working methods, with as many interruptions as possible, made fewer demands on our worn bodies and in this way helped to prolong our lives. Knowing the business inside out, I had the makings of quite a good saboteur.

The weak points on the Piestany production line were the five turntables at intervals along the sixty-yard tracks, which ran the length of the factory from the kilns where the tiles were fired at one end to the yard where they were loaded onto trucks at the other. The convicts from Leopoldov had been put to work manning the trolleys along the tracks between these points. Each convict pushed his trolley about a dozen yards to the next turntable, and so on down to the end of the line, where another group loaded the tiles onto waiting trucks. It was strenuous work, and for those manning the trolleys at the kiln end of the hangar it was also extremely hot.

Any delay on the trolley feedline from the kilns to the trucks naturally threw the entire production process out of kilter. The only obvious place for accidents to happen was at one of the five turntables, where subsidiary tracks joined the main line and the wheels of the trolleys temporarily left their otherwise stable grooves. The time when accidents most frequently occurred coincided with the time when we most wanted them to happen: in the afternoons, when the workers were beginning to tire. Some of the Leopoldov team developed a very fine skill at staging these midafternoon accidents, blessing the factory's entire work force with as much as an hour's idleness.

Könyves, the works manager, would then emerge from his office and rush frantically up and down the line, shouting abuse at these criminal idiots who repeatedly held up his production. His noncriminal civilian staff, above suspicion, would stand on one side, smoking patiently, until the fault had been put to rights. They soon became used to these irregular breaks and were very sorry when our Piestany assignment came to an end. Inside the fortress, sabotage as blatant as this would have been punished with extreme severity, but out in the tranquil Slovakian countryside one could get away with almost anything. It was Könyves who had to take the blame, and he deserved to take the blame. He cheated us over our rations, pocketing half the subsidy that Leopoldov paid him for our lunches.

Toward the end of the Piestany assignment one of the men in our team fell ill and was replaced by a man called Zimmermann. The new man was a Pressburg Jew who told us he had been sentenced to six years for having worked in the former American consulate, but later I doubted the truth of these claims. He approached me one day in the factory and asked me if he could have a word with me during the lunch break. I agreed. At twelve o'clock we met in the yard.

"I am here to arrange your escape," said Zimmermann without further introduction, and asked me to follow him to the fence of the factory compound. I was too dumbfounded to do anything but obey.

"Over there," he continued, as we walked across the compound, "on the other side of the fence, you can see a road leading down into the valley, where it is out of sight. Over here, on this side of the fence, is the shed with the latrines. It's easy to climb onto the roof of the shed, and from there to jump over the fence. Your escape has been arranged for tomorrow. Just after midday you will see a black car come over the brow of the hill and drive slowly down into the valley, where it will stop and wait for as long as it takes you to get from the fence to the road — five minutes at the outside. Get into this car and ask no questions. You will be home within two days."

"And who are you?" I asked.

"Zimmermann," he said, and walked away.

I tried several times in the course of the afternoon to get Zimmermann on his own so that I could have another word with him, but he took pains to avoid me. I had no idea as to his real identity. Perhaps he *was* a helping friend, and in that case I didn't want to risk his neck.

I spent a sleepless night. What should I do? There would be no time to decide on the following day. I would have to make up my mind before morning. It sounded too good to be true: so it couldn't be true. How could Zimmermann have smuggled himself into Leopoldov without the connivance of the Czech authorities? And if they were in on the plan, then it was probably a trap. But why would they want to set a trap? To have a pretext for keeping me longer in the country? They could do that in any case. Suppose not a trap, then. Suppose an honest proposal, at the intervention of some foreign power in a position to plant agents in the most closely guarded prison in the country. Without knowledge of the Czechoslovakian government. For, surely, if the Czechs agreed to let me out, then the matter could be arranged much more simply, without clandestine meetings and black cars. They need only release me and send me back home. An arranged escape then, the real thing. Should I risk it? Be home in two days instead of in three years. Three years of my life, my family, my freedom! But even if it were the real thing: what if the plan went wrong? How many extra years for a failed escape? Five? Ten? Ten possible against three certain years. And so I arrived at the worst possible conclusion: I decided to wait and see.

The following morning there was no sign of Zimmermann among the convicts waiting in the prison yard. Where was my fifteenth man, I asked the warder who was checking our numbers. He told me I'd have to do without a fifteenth man that day; the replacement had reported sick. Fifteenth man: that was what did it. I didn't like that number. I'd once been a fifteenth man myself. By the time I climbed up into the truck I had made up my mind that I wouldn't go. I'd stay on the side of the fence I knew.

As soon as the midday siren sounded in Piestany I made my way over to the shed and shut myself in one of the latrines. Through the window I could see the fence, and beyond the fence the brow of the hill and the road down into the valley. I held my breath and counted.

About a minute and a half after noon I saw a black limousine appear on the crest of the hill and cruise down into the valley. I couldn't believe my eyes. A minute passed. It was true. I tore the door open, closed it again, sat down on the toilet seat. And there I stayed for the next half hour, unable to act or even think, utterly numb, until a dull feeling inside me unraveled and articulated itself with painful clarity: three years of my free life had just passed down the road and out of sight while I sat in the latrines of the Piestany tileworks.

Had they? I never found an answer. I never saw or heard of Zimmermann again.

*   *   *

It took Boros a month to get from Leopoldov to Budapest. It took him a morning to get back.

Boros remained only briefly in the fortress. For six weeks he was chained to the wall in its very authentic dungeons, the dreaded *Kasematten,* before being returned to the district court prison in Pressburg, where he was put on trial. I lost track of him after his departure for Pressburg, but we were able to piece together an account of how Boros had spent his ten weeks of freedom.

For several days he had wandered southeast through the Slovakian countryside, avoiding the roads, eating wild strawberries and sleeping out. At first the weather was mild. Then followed days of uninterrupted rain. The temperatures suddenly dropped. Exhausted, soaked through and through, he knocked on a farmhouse door one evening. The farmer's wife opened the door. The sight of this man with his shredded clothes and shorn convict's head terrified the poor woman. Boros remained standing on the doorstep until he was invited inside. He explained in his modest, most courteous manner that he was a Hungarian priest who had been jailed in Pressburg because of his anti-Communist teachings. He was now on his way home. Could he dry his clothes at her fire and have a bite to eat? Whether it was the artful ploy of calling himself a priest, or another, less priestly fascination that he had always exerted on women, the farmer's wife was soon won over and, wiping her hands on her apron, she invited Father Boros to step inside.

He spent the next ten days in bed with a fever. The farmer nursed him with hot broth, his wife with cold poultices. Apparently they were used to conspiracy. Their two sons had been partisans; both had been caught and shot in 1944 while they were still in their teens. Between broth and poultice the rascally but still religious Boros said masses for their souls. In the meantime his irresistible hair again began to curl on his scalp, the old sparkle rekindled in his eyes. The farmer's wife said what a pity it was for such a fine fellow to be wasted on a priest, and immediately crossed herself for her blasphemy. Boros saw that it was time to be moving on. The farmer fitted him out in his dead son's clothes and took him in his cart to the neighboring town of Komorn. Here the old man revived his fading partisan connections to obtain for Boros a discreet berth on one of the Danube barges plying between Pressburg and Budapest. In the midsummer of 1950 Boros returned in triumph to his native city along the same route by which his former business associate had so unceremoniously left it.

Boros wasted no time. By lunchtime the penniless bargee had become the owner of several wallets, by teatime the bargee had disappeared inside the elegant suit of a city gentleman, who by eight o'clock that evening had been elevated to a candlelit dinner table in the most expensive hotel in town. The extravagant guest disregarded coarse linen napkins, wiping his lips on the corners of a silk handkerchief instead, preferred to light his cigars with tapers of screwn-up banknotes, ignoring the matches the waiters proffered him, and displayed a restless occupation with the incongruously military cut of his hair. Even by the standards of the establishment, proletarian postwar Budapest had not seen the likes of Boros for a very long time.

The hotel guest attracted attention. On his way out the next morning he was intercepted in the foyer and reminded that he had not yet complied with a request to show the documents necessary for his registration. Boros apologized, stepped back into the elevator to fetch his papers, prudently descended by way of the house staff stairs, and sought the safety of the lunchtime crowds via a convenient backstreet tradesmen's entrance. Clearly there would be problems with hotels and their tiresome regulations. Boros began to look around for other accommodation.

The solution to the problem of alternative sleeping arrangements most naturally presented itself to him in the shape of a woman. His ingenious mind began to devise a hard-luck story. After he had been walking for half an hour or so Boros conceded that his plan would entail parting with his newly acquired suit, and so his steps reluctantly led him back to the pawnshop near the Danube wharf where only yesterday he had arrived. Under the pawnbroker's suspicious eyes the prince reverted to the frog. In came today's gentleman, out went yesterday's bargee.

Ex-convict, abdicated prince, currently bargee with portering ambitions, Boros posted himself at the railway station where for a few days he carried eligible bags and hailed taxis in which he watched his hopes disappear. He spent his nights under one of the Danube bridges. But one morning, among the luggage that descended from the Kiev train, he could feel in his hands the soft leather grip of a bag that gave a distinctly responsive tug. There were five bags in all and each, although heavier, was more charming than the last. The muscle of Boros received the support of a heart that listened sympathetically to his story. He toiled and talked, his instincts wide awake. Bags vaulted from the platform onto his willing cart. They seemed reluctant to leave his capable hands. Boros charmed jostling crowds to part, taxis to materialize at empty curbs, and in no time at all was negotiating five flights of stairs that led up to an unfurnished apartment on the other side of the river.

A lot needed to be done to the apartment, beginning with the front door, which fell off its hinges by way of welcome. Five upcoming bags, now mute with disappointment, waited heavily on the threshold; their collective heart sank. The versatile Boros modestly offered his services as joiner, painter, electrician and furnisher general. It did not matter that he could supply none of these services himself. He could find and harness them for a complete overhaul of the apartment within two weeks. The bags again sprang lightly into his hands, made their way back down five flights of stairs and into a nearby hotel. A hand explored the pockets of a dress, which only now appeared to Boros to be unnecessarily stern on such an attractive wearer, thought better of the coins it found there, and shyly offered itself instead. How could she thank him? Boros could think of many ways, but for the time being he kept that to himself.

The next two weeks saw rapid progress in the derelict apartment on the far side of the river and in the heart of the young lady who had arrived to take possession of it. The interior decorator responsible for these changes, working against the feverish instincts of his blood, eased himself slowly, casually, into the possession of both. Boros, whose warnings about the risk of housebreakers were not inspired by chivalry alone, volunteered to remain on the premises to guard them at night. His suit advanced with the furnishings, from bare boards to carpeted floors, from carpets to a submissive couch, from the couch to a passionate christening of a newly delivered, still-unsheeted bed too impatient to wait longer for its mistress's body. Boros awoke from a five-year sleep and found himself on a cloud in heaven, with a view down over gradually descending rooftops to the immortal Danube in the distance.

He disregarded the Russian origins of the train that had brought him this waking dream, he overlooked the severe style of the clothes that were filling the wardrobe in front of his eyes, overheard undreamlike words such as fascist, exile, revolutionary cause, because Boros had never known any women who talked this way; and such was his foolishness, his vanity, or perhaps his mere happiness, that a gradual sharpening of the contours of the sumptuous presence beside him in the sheets went unremarked. And what cause did he have to be suspicious? He knew that her family had escaped to Kiev in the war. Nothing could be more natural: Boros had spent his whole life escaping and regarded it as the human condition. She had returned to Hungary. So had he. She was employed as a secretary in some ministry, but he took no interest in her work except when it inconvenienced his own desires. She was always writing, writing, writing. Sometimes he would wake in the night and see her writing by flashlight, a pad on her knee. He scolded her industry, hiding the pad under his pillow. But he never asked to see what she was writing. Boros was too proud to admit that he had never learned to read. She loved him nonetheless, did she not? Only his senses could have told him, could have transmitted through his literate fingers the braille messages of his lover's skin. And suppose she herself had told him: would he, even then, have understood the shock, the sudden, irreversible freezing of her soul? How could Boros have ever guessed that he paid for his daytime happiness with a final subterranean purge, six years after the event, in a succession of dreadful nights? Not mere talking in his sleep. I was witness. A man's conscience could sit him bolt upright, still embalmed in the shroud of sleep, could put on his boots and walk him up and down, up and down, put a shovel in his hands to clear the corpses from his path, battered children, severed limbs. Boros awoke refreshed. He never saw these terrible pantomimes of his sleep. Bad enough for me, who liked him, on a pallet beside him in Leopoldov. But for her, who had thought she loved him and shared his bed: it stopped her heart. She began to record the confessions of his sleep. The dictation went on for many nights. Much of it was incoherent. She transcribed the remainder on her typewriter keys. It amounted to no more than a couple of pages in the end. She turned her report in and told Boros what she had done. Boros was stunned. The police were waiting for him downstairs. She followed him down. When he arrived in the district court prison in Pressburg Boros told his fellow prisoners his story. He said he had been betrayed. And so he had. He had betrayed himself.

When I had finished polishing Quitt's accounts for him I was transferred to the prison's needlework department as a cloth cutter. Thanks to this job, which assured an inexhaustible supply of scraps of material, my sixty-odd cellmates spent the winter of 1950 with warm feet. The shrinkage of shirts and blankets came to an end; quiltwork decorations illuminated gray pallets. And meanwhile a conspiracy of needles continued to rise and dip in silence, rise and dip over a very much larger, more difficult patchwork. It was a task for five men: two Slovaks, a Pressburg-born American, and two Germans, known to their exclusive needle circle as Bottom and Top. They were planning an escape.

A lot of thread went into this work, not only the thread for the rope ladder to be slung over Leopoldov's walls, but for the fine strands spanning the thousands of miles of a web that would reach from Bratislava to Pittsburgh on the other side of the Atlantic Ocean. And for me, watching the needles rise and dip, there would also be far-reaching consequences, although I had aided the escapers with no more than my thoughts and refused to entrust myself to ladders of any kind.

Cernak, one of the two Slovaks, was the leader of the

team. Like hundreds of others whom I met in prison at this time he had been jailed on the standard charge of anti-Communist activities. He was a relative of Matus Cernak, who served as minister under Benes and Tiso and was later assassinated in exile. It was Cernak, always wary of Czechs, particularly when they had been bribed, who succeeded in arranging for a sympathetic warder to be brought into Leopoldov from outside at a time when Slovak staff were otherwise being eased out of the prison administration. This warder provided Cernak with the set of seven keys necessary for his escape and made all the outside arrangements — forged papers, transport, and money. Because of the time involved in making these arrangements, secrecy was absolutely essential, and Cernak accordingly invited only a small group of men whom he knew and trusted to make his escape with him. Although I was not an original member of his team I knew all the details of the escape, because for a couple of months I happened to be cloth cutter to Cernak and his conspiratorial sewers at the same workshop bench.

The coordination of the movements of the five escapers posed a problem. With the exception of the two Slovaks they were all quartered in different cells. Prisoners were not allowed watches, but if they stood by the windows they could hear the chimes of the church clock in the village about a mile away. The escape was planned for midnight. Here the first four of Cernak's seven keys would be required: one for himself and his fellow Slovak, one for the American, one each for the two Germans. The first rendezvous for the Slovaks and the American was arranged for the east corridor, onto which their cell doors opened, and for the west corridor in the case of the two Germans. Cernak kept all the keys, in a cache known only to himself, until the day of the escape. On that day the American and the two Germans would be given the key to their respective cells before they returned from work. Cernak's fifth key was a key to the duplicate locks on the doors leading from the west and the east corridors onto the intermediate passage, running from north to south and patrolled by two armed guards who would have to be put out of action. These two guards worked separately, one checking the cells along the west corridors, the other the cells along the east corridors. It was impossible to know in advance where the guards would be at midnight, because patrols were carried out at irregular intervals. The safest solution, it seemed to Cernak, was not to trust their luck and make a run for it but to minimize the risk by deliberately drawing the guards to the point where they could most easily be eliminated; and the obvious point for that was where their east-west corridor met at the main passage. The two Germans would make a commotion to attract the guards; Cernak and his friends would be waiting behind an already unlocked door just across the way. As soon as the guards came to investigate, the Cernak team would jump them from behind. Cernak would then open the door and let the Germans into the main passage. His sixth key gave them admittance to one of the inner courtyards. No problems there — the gate was unguarded. The seventh key opened the gate to the main courtyard at the back of the prison. Directly behind this gate stood a sentry box, manned by a raucous old warder who would either be drunk or asleep: Cernak's helper would see to that. The escapers had now arrived at the ramparts and a thirty-foot drop to freedom on the other side of the fortress walls. But of course nobody would be dropping, for that afternoon the Germans would have smuggled an unusual two-piece undersuit, very fine and very strong, from the workshop into their cells. Unhurried, oblivious to the cold, and methodical as only Germans are,

Bottom and Top would now undress, respectively taking off the lower and upper halves of a thirty-foot rope ladder for their companions to attach and throw over the wall. A car would be waiting outside the village, and if all went well the desperadoes would be in a safe house in Bratislava before dawn.

There was only one thing that I was not allowed to know: the actual night of the escape. Even the escapers themselves received only twenty-four hours' warning. But Cernak's obsessive secrecy paid off. I never noticed when Bottom and Top put on their versatile underwear, never heard any untoward noises at midnight. I only heard recriminations two days, saw bandaged heads two weeks after the escapers had gone. Alone now at my cutter's table in the corner of the workshop, I did however realize what a compromising position I had been left in, how conspicuous my claims of ignorance. No doubt most of the prisoners hoped for Cernak and his friends that they would never return to Leopoldov, but probably I was the only one who prayed.

At least I prayed with warm feet. The winter froze and thawed under extravagantly lined boots. Already it was March. Thonet's lime trees would soon be in bud. No news; good news. Around the middle of the month I celebrated an anniversary: not the four years I had already spent in prison, but the two years more before I left it. A few days later Cernak returned to Leopoldov.

Cernak's return took place in total secrecy, but within a very short time the news had seeped through the porous prison walls. What had happened?

After arriving in Bratislava the escapers had split up into three groups: the two Slovaks, the two Germans, and the American on his own. Different border crossings had been planned for each of the three groups; the American traveled south to Yugoslavia via Hungary, the Germans north to the Bavarian border west of Pilsen. Cernak didn't know what happened to them. He never saw them again. He and his companion took the shortest route west. Within three days of leaving Leopoldov they were sitting in a consulate in Vienna being interrogated by the Americans, to whom they had applied for citizenship.

And here something extraordinary happened: Cernak agreed to return to Czechoslovakia as an American agent. Whether he agreed to this madness in exchange for his citizenship remained unclear — I never learned the details. Whatever his reasons, Cernak came back, resurfacing in Bratislava only a few weeks after he had left it. He must have underestimated the opposition the second time around. He was no longer playing cops and robbers with the sleepy Slovakian police; he was up against the national security agents from Prague. It didn't take the professionals long to catch him. Perhaps it was merely for administrative reasons that they brought Cernak back to Leopoldov at all, because he now belonged to a category of prisoner for whom there could be only one destination: the notorious state security prison, Ruzyn, located conveniently close to Prague Airport. In Leopoldov Cernak was given a foretaste of what awaited him in Ruzyn. Among the facts that were painfully extracted from him during his brief visit was the name of a certain Joseph Pallehner, not an accessory to the escape, oh no, he would have no part in it, just a cutter of the cloth that five pairs of needles had shaped.

The cloth cutter was summoned from his workbench. Did 6413 know a prisoner by the name of Cernak? Which Cernak? He knew half a dozen men by the name of Cernak. The Cernak who had escaped. Escape? Never heard of any escape. Idiot! Prisoner 6413 had conspired to escape and was sentenced herewith to one month's confinement in the *Kasematten*.

It could have come worse than that, I thought to myself. Four weeks in the dungeon, out of a maximum sentence of six. And no formal hearing, no additional sentence to be served: just the same time spent even less agreeably than it would otherwise have been. And so with a feeling almost of relief I was marched away to have my irons fitted in the prison smithy.

How natural that already sounded: to have my irons fitted! This was in the year of our Lord one thousand nine hundred and fifty, in a country that had allegedly enjoyed a quite considerable period of civilization and had itself been only recently freed from the yoke of a barbarous oppressor. What had been learned? In the fortress smithy nothing had been learned. The forge where I watched my shackles being beaten out on the anvil was authentically medieval. I was required to undress: once the fetters had been attached to my feet there could be no more removal of trousers. I found myself encased in an obscene garment, specially manufactured for the purpose; knee-length breeches, buttoned from the knees to the groin so that a man artifically impeded could perform what nature required of him. The length of chain between my ankles was enough for a labored shuffle, not enough to descend upright the flight of steps that led to the dungeons. I was permitted to crawl downstairs. And now I left the light behind me, advancing slowly down a fading tunnel into absolute darkness.

What happens to a man deprived of light, deprived of sound and all record of time? His senses are not extinguished, by no means. They redouble and rebound on him. They hurry out into a barren surrounding, canvass the emptiness for accustomed perceptions, find nothing; falter; return discredited, self-perplexed. Again and again, in an exhausting cycle. Sometimes I thought I heard silence. Sometimes I heard nothing. The distinction between the two was very fine; a borderline that my sense of hearing crossed and recrossed, as many times in as many seconds, with a kind of spontaneous, uncontrollable jump. Now it was here, now it was gone.

It was impossible for my senses to be awake and busy, as waking senses have no option but to be, and to endure enforced redundancy at the same time. Before long they would have driven me out of my mind. It was likewise not possible to live timelessly. My very organism was a succession of events, a finite number of heartbeats, a finite division of cells. I could not deny myself time. And so it occurred to me to reproduce outside my body the ceaseless activity that took place within it. In the timeless void that threatened to draw me into its own extinction I would project the evidence establishing my senses and my personal measure of time. Ceaseless activity, back and forth, up and down. I heard steps, I counted them, lost count. Silence was when I stopped moving. My senses were restored to order, my sanity assured.

I found I had cause to be grateful for the invention of gunpowder. The storage of powder required dryness, and munitions had once been stored in Leopoldov's dungeons. The former magazine, although cool, kept its prisoners as dry as it had its powder. The floor seemed to be made of some closely packed substance, probably sand. Standing rooted in the sand, not peering into but peered into by the darkness, my body having lost all its visible boundaries, not sweating, preserved in this cool, dry, dark climate, I sometimes felt like a shriveled plant stored in a cellar during the winter months. And meanwhile, plantlike, I survived on a slow, imperceptible pulse, and waited for someone to come and take me out.

I learned the unusual geography of my cell. It was shaped like a triangle, the door at its base, toward the inside of the fortress. The star-shaped structure one saw above ground continued all the way down to the foundations; that explained why my cell was triangular. The journey from the door to the corner opposite where two converging walls met was a journey to the end of the world: no farther, deeper, or darker than this. I had reached the bottom. I really had. Shuffling around in the dark. Harder to keep my balance in the dark: a blind animal on its hind legs. Food was tossed onto the floor for me, like an animal. I was beaten for sport, like an animal. I crouched on my haunches and did my dirt in a corner, like an animal. What more can I say? It was far worse than anything I had ever imagined.

Somewhere there must have been a ventilation shaft. I could not see it, but I could feel an upward motion of the air. This air shaft buoyed up my hopes, I don't know why. I spoke my hopes out loud. It carried them back above ground.

And then a door opened. Remained open. The darkness rushed out. Elsewhere a month had passed, but I knew I had been away for many years. For the first time I experienced the agony of light. I had to wear a shield over my eyes. I was restored to trousers. I ceased to be an animal. But I continued to rot. Skin flaked from my ears and the lids of my eyes. I was very ill. I was taken to the infirmary. The doctor told me I had pneumonia, and maybe I had, but that was not what was wrong with me. My illness was not something I had, but something I had become. It was a sickness of life, and it was not a sickness that anyone would be able to cure until I had become, once again, a free man.

The Great Wheel

Having surfaced from darkness to abrupt daylight I remained in the prison infirmary for several weeks, suspended in what seemed to be a twilight of my own feverish mind but was in fact real and not imagined, a condition of the infirmary itself. The sick were quartered in the original monastery buildings, where their ability to survive, like the piety of the monks who had once inhabited the same cells, was not so much encouraged as challenged by the deprivation of light. Gashes in the wall, not windows but wounds on the outside world, made a reluctant admission to daylight, and to a daylight that was already confined, teased through the maze of surrounding prison walls to the last of many inner courts, to the heart of the labyrinth itself.

From far away I heard voices, voices that remained indistinct even when the speakers were bending over me and I felt a pain in my side. Sometimes I heard them clearly; it seemed to be a trick of how I held my head. To my surprise I recognized Sellner, whom I had not seen since the night of our arrival at police headquarters in Bratislava. I asked him what they were doing to me. We are drawing water off your lungs, he said. Water off my lungs? Can't you get it out of my ears instead? But Sellner must have thought I was delirious, and put a cold compress on my legs to bring down the fever. The damp cloths made me shudder. They came every day to draw water off my lungs, and whenever I asked them to get it out of my ears they put a cold compress on my legs instead. I could make no sense of it. Sometimes I would hear them say "Half a liter on this side," and sometimes they appeared to remain behind a silent boundary of speech, audible only to themselves, for although I saw the lips of the speaker move I could no longer hear what he said. Sellner came and went and tended my body with gentle hands. I remembered that I had saved his life and realized that he was now helping to save mine.

Gradually the tide retreated from my lungs and the fever cooled, leaving a sensation of parched stillness in the body it had exhausted. I continued to hear voices, however, even when no one was there; not a normal voice but a hollow, disembodied whispering, and not from a source but in a spiral, tripping over its own resonances as it circled the walls of my cell. I explained this voice outside my body as a projection of its mute, still-feverish awareness of the destruction it had only just survived, of its resurrection, then, for why else did I always hear the same disinterred syllables: Lazarus, Lazarus? Wasn't I the Lazarus, announcing the miracle to himself? And I continued to indulge in the comfort of this absurd thought until one evening, for the first time gingerly lowering my legs to explore the floor with the soles of my feet, I heard someone cough and curse into my ear as if he had been only a foot away. I withdrew my legs instantly and peered cautiously under the bed.

"Who are you?"

"Ah! You can hear me at last. I've been trying to get you for some time. Feeling better?"

"Thank you. But where on earth are you?" I echoed in astonishment.

"Two cells down from you. Pleased to make your acquaintance at last. My name is Tibor Lazar."

"Lazar!"

It was in these unusual circumstances that I shook off the specter of the grave and made the acquaintance not of Lazarus but of Tibor Benjamin Lazar.

The sepulchral voice of my cell neighbor was conveyed to me through a section of disused water pipe, which for some reason had not been removed but merely sawn off and concealed behind a ventilation grid in the corner opposite my bed. My pleasure on being introduced to Tibor Lazar's company in this original way was unfortunately marred by a painful discovery. When I sat on the side of my bed with my head between my knees, as I had been at the moment Lazar happened to cough, I could hear him as distinctly as if he had been sitting beside me, but when I turned the left side of my head toward the ventilation grid his voice became distant, almost inaudible. I had become deaf in my left ear. It was with the right side of my head turned to that corner of my cell that I listened to the confidences emanating from the water pipe and to everything else the world would say to me, for the remainder of my life.

I had lost track of time. Tibor told me it was the tenth of June, 1951. I had been brought to the infirmary six weeks ago. Tibor himself had been incarcerated in the infirmary since his arrival in Leopoldov in February, although there was nothing wrong with him. His captors had assigned him to the infirmary, Tibor said cryptically, not because he was a sick man but in order for him to become one. And they would be proved right, he added, if only because they had time on their side. He had been sentenced to life imprisonment "for playing cards."

Playing cards was Tibor's euphemism for his close friendship with Vladimir Clementis, Ladislav Novomesky, and other leading Slovak Communists who had fallen from grace with the Soviets and the Soviet-controlled government in Prague. Tibor was a cynical man, investing his cynicism in a euphemistic manner of speech whose mood I found it difficult to gauge. He was a Pressburg-trained lawyer who had practiced in Brünn and Prague and had been "in recess" in London during the war, where he had associated with the group of Czechoslovakian exiles around Benes. But the friendships formed at this time, notably with Clementis, were "merely personal and politically nonaligned." He was not a political man; it was his misfortune to live in a political age.

After the war he returned to private practice in Pressburg, watching with equanimity the elevation of the Londoners to office and power. But he continued to meet them socially, playing skat with a set of political acquaintances that perceptibly began to dwindle after the Communist coup in February 1948. Tibor regretted the arrival on the scene of a new breed of politicians who did not play cards, for it had been his experience that when political opponents could sit down at a common card table this continued to exert a civilizing influence on them after they had left it. Thus the fascist collaborator Stano Mach, as Tiso's minister of the interior, had held a decidedly better hand in 1941 than the Slovak nationalists Husak and Novomesky, but he had played his cards to his opponents' advantage, saving them from imprisonment and trial. And how other than as an acknowledgment of the debt of the card player who has been bailed out could their intervention five years later be explained, when they held all the aces and Mach none, and at a cost of thirty years' hard labor had snatched him from the extinction of the ultimate debt collector? Novomesky visited Mach in Leopoldov, where they resumed their game of cards. Tibor noted that Tuka, Mach's colleague at the Ministry of Foreign Affairs and by contrast not a card player, but otherwise not more villainous than Mach, had been condemned to death. His successor as foreign minister fared no better, for in Tibor's view it had been the secret objective of the February coup to oust the card players, and those, like Masaryk, who briefly survived, survived only as a threatened species in an environment that had ceased to respect the card player's code of fair play. Masaryk disappeared. To Tibor's horror, his old acquaintance from the London years, Vladimir Clementis, was appointed in Masaryk's place. Observing the high incidence of political mortality among his skat partners, he felt that the least he could do was to represent their interests in his professional capacity as a lawyer.

Throughout 1949 he defended a flush of Democrats, bishops, and trade unionists, all former players, in an unequal match against opponents who did not hesitate to mark cards or to interpret the rules to their advantage. By the end of that year Tibor had lost all his skat partners and by the middle of the next year all his clients. In March 1950 the anniversary of Masaryk's demission was marked by the dismissal of Clementis, and at the ninth congress of the Slovak Communist Party held in the spring the graves of the "bourgeois nationalists" that had been dug two years previously were at last assigned specific occupants: Clementis, Smidke, Husak and Novomesky, among many others. As a preliminary to the dismantling of their reputations (for they had all been distinguished leaders of wartime resistance) the offenders were summarily removed from their posts. Some of them would soon be removed from life, others would escape the graves for which they were intended. Tibor sat alone in his chambers and laid games of patience, counting knaves and clubs. In the summer he followed the course of the trial of prominent Democrats, where a good deal of bluff and trumpery led to some very sharp practice indeed: nine long terms of imprisonment and four death sentences. In the winter he witnessed the same spectacle repeated under the more diverting title of the Trial of the Agents of the Vatican in Czechoslovakia. Tibor kept a count of the toll, transfixing to the walls of his chambers an obituary ace of hearts for every death sentence passed by the State Courts since the February coup. Within four years, had he stayed in his chambers, he would have counted over two hundred. But Tibor did not finish his collection. At his trial it was even cited as evidence of the plaintiff's bourgeois degeneracy and unsoundness of mind. He was found guilty of anti-Communist activities and entrusted to the infirmary of Leopoldov for the regeneration of his mental health.

For a man who claimed to be nonpolitical, Tibor was excellently informed, even after spending months in solitary confinement. This was because of his frequent "business trips" to Bratislava, Ruzyn and Prague, where he assisted the security police with their enquiries. It was in this way that he learned of the arrest of Husak and Novomesky in February 1951 and of the new accusations brought against them at a session of the Central Committee in April. He told me that he did not expect Husak and Novomesky to be put on trial for some time, as the documentation of the case against them appeared to involve "unusual efforts." He assumed that in the meantime they had also been accommodated in Leopoldov, but evidently in such secrecy that he was unable to confirm his suspicions. Before it came to Husak's and Novomesky's turn he was convinced that another important trial would be staged around a second group, involving Clementis, that much he knew, although Clementis himself was probably not the principal in whose honor it would be held.

One evening Tibor's sepulchral whisper roused me from a deep sleep. "Joseph! Joseph!"

I swung my legs over the side of the bed and leaned forward toward the ventilation grid.

"Ah. There you are. Did I wake you? I have something on my mind . . ."

An indescribable sigh, like one of Tibor's languid euphemisms, traveled down the pipe between us and curled up at my feet.

"Would I have done better to marry, Joseph? Have I wasted my life? Or would it have been wasted for me, regardless, without my doing? I find a certain consolation in my present circumstances. The apathy is enforced, and thus I am absolved of responsibility for my natural condition. But this is not what I meant to talk about. . . ."

Tibor cleared his throat, and the pipe noisily amplified it, of these unwanted stoppages, and continued on a brisker note.

"Only recently have I come to appreciate the irony of the fact that Kafka was a citizen of Prague."

"What's ironical about that?"

"Well, I now understand that he was in effect an advance undercover agent of our State Security Police. Well ahead of his time he prepared a comprehensive dossier expounding, in merely speculative terms, that theory of *the inversion of the crime and the indictment* which has begun to find practical application in our own generation. As a lawyer I have found it instructive to consider how such a monstrous proposal could ever have been brought to life and even, by the inoculation of habit, ceased to be regarded as a deformity at all.

"In retrospect it's clear that the transformation of the Kafka dossier from imagination to reality began with the Communist takeover in 1948. The Communists initiated it, but without, I believe, intending it or even being aware of quite what they were setting in motion. Agitation, provocation, polemical liquidation of the enemy, the occasional assassination — all this was the usual fare to which one had unfortunately long since become accustomed. Even the early political trials of Ursiny and the postwar Democrats took place in accordance with the jaded maxim that the right is with the power. Which is bad enough.

"Nobody seeks actively to implement the Kafka dossier, however, because of the arbitrariness of the power that it envisages. It is an uncontrollable power, being an unidentifiable power. It is implemented nonetheless; it implements itself. This process seems to have been facilitated by the confusion of administrative competence. Apparently the Communists have not yet consolidated their power bases equally in all the organs of the state, for they are still at the stage of tolerating cooperation with certain opposition elements. In due course they will be weeded out, but even at this stage, you see, quite apart from the encumbrance of practical administration, the distinctions between friend and foe are already beginning to blur.

"The Communists in the State Security Service have found that they are unable to operate the mechanism of political trials as fully as they would like, because their victims are in the custody of a still independent judicature. They have been at liberty to instigate trial proceedings, not to control their outcome. Under these circumstances it could and did happen that the accused exploited the courtroom as a forum to discredit the motives of those who had conspired to bring him to trial. The Communists were accordingly obliged to act with restraint, and throughout 1948 and most of 1949 the weapon of the political trial was used rather sparingly.

"Until now they have been looking for real enemies. The enemies were there. They were conveniently marked with distinct political labels. When actual opposition came to an end the need for enemies did not thereby cease, however. A reappraisal of all self-professed Communists was called for, in the course of which it emerged that many were not Communists at all. What were they then? But of course any genuine enquiry was forestalled by the more pertinent question: what would the state find it desirable for them to be? Whatever it pleases. In this way the principle of framing the indictment prior to the offense and in anticipation of any actual offender has come to be established in the political system. But in what system? Who are its trustees? No longer the courts. The government? The party? The security organs?

"I have no answer, Joseph. Do you?"

"Perhaps there are no longer any trustees . . ."

"Perhaps. Let's console ourselves with the thought that it is easier to live in prison than in the fear of it. Good night, Joseph!"

In the wake of Tibor's voice I felt a rush of silence down the water pipe.

Not long afterwards Tibor must have been called away on one of his sudden business trips. He was absent for several months, and I became worried that he might never return. I missed him. Shut in the silence of my isolation again, I was troubled by a new anxiety: that perhaps Tibor had not gone, but that I had lost all capacity to hear him. I took to posting myself with my good ear to the door to listen for the sound of the hatch being shot back when the warder passed my food in to me, and I would often rap the door just to reassure myself of my hearing. Hadn't these sounds become fainter? Had I once heard them more distinctly? I tried to remember the sound of my knuckles on the door and to compare it with the sound I heard now, but I found I couldn't remember sounds in the way that I could remember images. This obsession with encroaching deafness reached such a pitch that it would have seriously affected the balance of my mind if I had not had the good fortune at this time to be assigned a job as orderly in the infirmary that released me from the ordeal of my isolation.

Outside my cell there were sounds and voices again, not of my own imagining, I could hear them unafraid, reassured that I had not lost my hearing altogether. Nonetheless, the world around me seemed to have become very still. I sterilized instruments, swabbed floors, changed linen, received my instructions, fetched and carried from one ward to another, snatched gossip from the mouths of my fellow orderlies, and all this activity seemed as if it were muffled under the soundproof glass of some vast, invisible dome. A dome of a kind was indeed there, not visible, but already palpable, for by this time the rumors that Leopoldov would shortly be taken over by the State Security Service had congealed into certain fact. The prison would thereby come under the direct administration of Prague. The foreknowledge alone dampened the warm spark in the relations between the inmates and their friendly Slovak guards and lowered the temperature inside the already chilly walls of the fortress a few degrees further.

In the infirmary the change of administration had already begun, and in some respects it brought an improvement. For the past few years the medical care of the prisoners had been entrusted to one of their fellow inmates, who had been obliged to improvise on his qualifications as a veterinary surgeon in order to treat human beings as successfully as he had animals in his previous career. The vet was replaced by a Czech doctor, who brought with him the more sophisticated equipment that the infirmary also badly needed. Until now operations had been carried out on an upturned packing case. Patients were etherized under gauze pads adapted from curtain material before coming under a scalpel that had been crudely forged in the prison smithy and whetted by the barber. Sellner had undergone operations on his hemorrhoids and appendix under these primitive conditions, apparently without ill effect.

Sellner had become even more gaunt and sallow-complexioned than I remembered him from our last meeting four years previously. After his trial in Banska Bystrica at the end of 1947 he had been transferred to Leopoldov, where within a few months he contracted tuberculosis and was isolated in a wing of the infirmary. He spent two years in isolation, at first alone and then in a cell with a fellow tubercular patient who was an old friend of mine, Count Esterhazy, erstwhile leader of the Hungarian lobby in the wartime Slovakian parliament. I asked Sellner eagerly for news of my old friend.

Sellner shook his head.

"Janos is dying. It's a hopeless case. Cough, cough, cough, all day and all night. His body is turning into a liquid he must spit out of his lungs. I'm afraid he won't last long."

I later learned that Esterhazy did in fact survive this prediction of his imminent death by six years. Unfortunately so, I feel bound to add, because they can only have prolonged the somber chronicle of illness and imprisonment that he had already suffered.

"He was arrested because of his political activities during the war," Sellner told me, "imprisoned on Russian orders in Pressburg and extradited to a labor camp behind the Arctic Circle. There he disappeared for several years. The Benes government intervened with the Soviets on his behalf, but were unable to get him out, and the Communist government subsequently condemned him to death, but were unable to get him hanged. Esterhazy showed up out of nowhere one day and was shoved over the Czech border. There he was, back home again. The Russians had sentenced him to ten years but he didn't serve the full time. The Czechs made amends for what the Russians had omitted and immediately put him back in jail. They revoked the death sentence, perhaps because they knew that nature had already procured him another. He will die here of tuberculosis instead. And he will die unnecessarily, because the medical treatment that could help him to recover has deliberately been withheld. The waste! As fine a man as ever I met. I could not even resent his coughing, although it kept me awake every night. There was only one thing I couldn't stand: the noise he made when he ate. Not his fault, poor fellow. Can you imagine the sight of a man mashing a crust with his bare gums? The nerves of one's own teeth grind in sympathy in their sockets. Of course his gums are as hard as bone. He got no fruit or vegetables at all during the years in Russia, you see, and so he contracted scurvy. All his teeth dropped out. An aristocrat crouching on the side of his bed, smacking his lips and mouthing his crusts like a monkey. To see Esterhazy like that is to be confronted with the ruin of Europe, no less. And none of us will fare much better. We'll never get out of here alive."

I reminded Sellner that he had once said the same thing to me before. Hadn't he survived the train journey from Pilsen to Pressburg? And his own death sentence? Sellner bit his lip. Perhaps his pessimism was understandable, for even though he had managed to cling onto the privilege of life he had not so far enjoyed any of its benefits. He was now thirty-one, and almost half his life had accomplished no more than his bare survival. For the past thirteen years he had been either a soldier or a prisoner, a young man who had never had a youth, who had lost his home and acquired nothing but experiences he would have done better without.

For several months we worked together as orderlies in the infirmary. Although Sellner had recovered from his long illness he was still far from well. A kind doctor arranged for his discharge from the unhealthy atmosphere of the infirmary and had him transferred to the kitchen gardens, where he would be given a more wholesome occupation in the open air. We shook hands at the infirmary gates and I watched him walk across a courtyard from shadow into sunlight. That is how I like to remember Sellner, walking at last into the sunlight, more generally, perhaps, of a better life, for that was the last I saw of him.

The wet autumn was curtailed by a sudden early frost. October days crept by on tiptoe, shrank under the stark November sky and froze into a motionless winter solstice. Time stalled in darkness. Where motion seemed to cease, so too did light and sound. Again I experienced the withdrawal of stimulus from the hollows of my ears and eyes, and listened to my own emptiness. Through the frost-grained windows of the infirmary I saw shattered images of the outside world. Tibor had been gone three months. What was I looking for? For confirmation, perhaps, some explanation outside my window for the deathliness inside, a brittle hush, suspended in the corridors and the ordinance rooms, that shivered under my feet like fragile ice. I did not remember the winter as cold as this. The change in climate was accompanied by a mysterious issue of rubber-soled footwear to the infirmary staff, a precaution taken not out of respect for the patients' need for silence, of which they already had quite enough, but because it facilitated a more discreet approach and thus a marginal benefit of surprise when visiting patients in their cells. With temperatures approaching zero, calculations of this nature became very fine. My errands to many of these cells were abruptly suspended. I did not need to ask the reason why, for although I never met the occupants I was well acquainted with their names.

My activities much reduced, through no fault of my own, I hurried up and down corridors, from one ordinance room to another, in pursuit of a sham industry that would keep me out of my cell. One day an ominous slogan had appeared on the infirmary walls. *Whoever does not work shall eat nothing and whoever does shall eat little.* Anyone contemplating the offense of idleness had now been forewarned. Staring hungrily at the letters E-A-T, I was surprised by the discovery of a memory that had been lost in me for almost five years: an image of a slice of bread and honey I had left uneaten on the table on the morning of my arrest. Could it be true? Was it possible for any man, ever, even a man with food crammed up to his gullet, to be guilty of such stupendous complacency as to refuse a slice of bread and honey? How could I have failed to lay in a stock for the lean times? My stomach groaned. Had I eaten it then I would surely be less hungry now. Nothing in all these years caused me such remorse as the memory of that slice of bread I had left uneaten.

There was less food now, and less became still less. A spartan regimen came to be enforced that bore an unmistakably military stamp. Orderlies moved at the double at all times. Prison staff had to be saluted. Gossip in the ordinance rooms was forbidden, penalties for disobedience were stepped up. Parades for all inmates were carried out in the freezing corridors three times a day. The entire staff of the infirmary was replaced. Before Christmas the change of administration we had been dreading had finally taken place.

The secret police had arrived in Leopoldov.

I had been expecting the summons, but it jolted me nonetheless. With the arrival of the new administration all cases were to be brought up for review. Why should it be my privilege to escape attention? Cells that had been inhabited yesterday were empty today, their inmates departed, like some of my fellow orderlies, for unknown destinations. A few days before Christmas I was called out of the surgery where I was unpacking supplies and taken to the same committee room in which I had been interviewed three years previously.

As we set out across the courtyard I wet my trousers in fear. The discomfort made me walk in an awkward, bowlegged fashion that caught the guard's attention.

"What have you got inside your trousers?" he asked suspiciously.

"Nothing."

"Then why are you walking like that?"

"My legs are stiff."

The guard told me to lower my trousers. I stood shamefully in the snow, trousers around my ankles, while the guard peered under my shirttail and poked a finger into my boots.

I waited outside the committee room for several hours. It was warmer there than in the infirmary. Even my acute anxiety gradually succumbed to this unaccustomed warmth and at some point I must have dozed off.

"6413!"

Instantly I was awake.

Three men were waiting for me in the committee room.

One of them, presumably a stenographer, continued writing all the time I was there, his head bent over the table, so that I could not get a proper look at his face. Opposite the stenographer sat a man with a stack of files, reminding me of the American judge and the summary justice he had handed down from his dais on the occasion of my first court appearance. This man, too, leafed idly through a file that lay open in front of him, just as the judge had done. It had become a very much more substantial file, I noticed, which was a reflection of the five intervening years now assembled between its covers. At the head of the table, directly facing me, sat a third man in uniform, smoking cigarettes in a long cigarette holder, who was obviously the person in charge.

For some minutes after I had entered the room not a word was spoken. The man in uniform tilted his head and blew smoke thoughtfully at the ceiling. His colleague with the files continued to leaf through the pages of my life and the stenographer went on writing. I wondered what. So far nothing had been said for him to take down. A digest of the previous case, perhaps. It unsettled me.

The man in uniform abruptly asked: "Well, what is he?"

"His name is Joseph Pallehner."

"Not who. What."

"A German. A fascist collaborator."

"He is a pig."

"Capitalist exploiter, oppressor of the Slovakian people . . ."

"A pig!"

His voice rose in anger. The other man turned a page.

"And? The sentence?"

"Six years."

"Six years!"

"That was before the State Courts had —"

"A travesty! Our courts would have hung him!"

I noted that the man with the files remained quite unmoved by his superior's sudden flashes of anger, and it occurred to me that these outbursts might be staged with the purpose of intimidating me.

The exchange between the two men went on in this way for about a quarter of an hour, in total disregard of me, not even a single glance, as if I had not been present in the room. I found this neglect much more disconcerting than the abuse to which I was subjected, and thus I was caught off balance when the uniformed man suddenly turned to me and asked how long I had been an orderly in the infirmary.

About five months, I said.

Five months, so. What illness had I most often encountered during those five months?

Diseases of the lung, bronchial complaints. I had encountered some cases of dysentery and tuberculosis, quite a few more of pneumonia.

Fatalities?

Unfortunately, yes.

Unfortunately? Unfortunately for whom?

Unfortunate for the deceased.

Did I believe in God?

No.

In an afterlife?

No.

Then why this nonsense about unfortunate for the deceased?

I said nothing.

Did I believe in the pope?

I said I did not regard the pope as an object of belief.

As an object of authority?

The pope didn't concern me: I was not a Christian.

A Jew then? A pig?

Neither Jew nor pig nor Communist.
Was that an insinuation or an avowal?
An avowal.
Exactly how many fatalities?
One or two in the summer, two or three since the autumn,
I did not know exactly.
Was I saying there had been an increase in recent months?
There might have been a slight increase, I couldn't say.
I alleged an increase, then: attributable to what?
To the cold weather, perhaps.
Cold since when?
Since late September or early October.
Colder than in past years?
Yes.
What evidence for that?
Water frozen in the sinks.
Names of fatalities?
I recalled two names.
That was fewer names than fatalities: what of unnamed
fatalities?
I said I couldn't remember all the names.
Names of patients generally? Reliable memory for names?
Unreliable.
Memory for numbers?
Rather more reliable.
How many patients in the infirmary? Fifty?
More.
A hundred?
I couldn't say.
But more than fifty: had I counted them?
Not counted, just a rough reckoning.
What had been my duties as orderly?
Inventories, for the most part.

What inventories?

Inventories of linen, bedpans, medical and other supplies.

Number of bedpans a basis for rough reckoning of number of bedpan users, perhaps? For better than a rough reckoning? Closer to fifty or a hundred and fifty?

I couldn't say.

Names of patients hospitalized in the last five months?

I mentioned a few names.

Talk to the patients in question?

We had exchanged a few words.

What about?

The usual things that prisoners talk about.

Arrest? Trial? Sentence?

Those matters had been touched on too. The patient's condition. The food. The unusually cold weather.

Speculations as to onset and duration of cold weather?

Quite a few.

Expectations of an early thaw?

Not in our lifetime.

When did the prisoner expect his release?

On March the fourteenth, 1953.

Silence.

"Another fifteen months?"

This question came unexpectedly from the stenographer, who had not said a word until now. He even found it important enough to interrupt his writing and to look up at me for the first time.

"Slansky."

I hurried over to the corner of my cell and crouched down by the ventilation grid.

"It's Slansky they're after. Slansky, Svab, Clementis, Freika, Frank . . . Sling, Margolius, Reicin . . . Simone, Fischl, Geminder . . ."

Tibor's cracked voice shoveled the names into my ear like a pile of broken fragments.

"I don't know how many more. Engrave them on your memory, Joseph, for there is already a legion of the nameless who will never be remembered."

"And I have been trying to unremember names as fast as I can —" Tibor had got back that night. I told him that the security police had taken over the administration of the prison during his absence, and of my interview with them the previous morning.

"Then I'm afraid that not much time is left us for these conversations, Joseph. The significance of these new measures is clear. Leopoldov will be transformed into an exclusively political prison. The common criminals, and probably most of the political convictions prior to the February coup, will be moved elsewhere. Leopoldov will be sealed off, to ensure as complete a secrecy as possible, disappear from the map. . . . It's most unfortunate that you caught pneumonia, Joseph."

"What d'you mean?"

"Isn't it obvious? You have been keeping dangerous company in the infirmary, Joseph. You have seen and heard too much. This may be diagnosed as a relapse in your political health, which otherwise seemed so well on the way to recovery. . . ."

"I only have another fifteen months to serve. My wife and family —"

"You fool! Forget your wife and family! Forget those fifteen months!"

I was shocked by the violence of this outburst.

"I cannot forget my family, Tibor," I said quietly.

"And I say you must, for your own good. Cut off your past, forget your hopes! Hopes disappointed poison one's soul — expect the worst, if you want to survive!"

For several minutes we sat in silence, each of us occupied with his own thoughts. Tibor continued in a dispassionate voice that attempted to conceal the urgency of what he felt.

"Perhaps somewhere in the vast archives of the state there is a piece of paper concerning a certain Joseph Pallehner, a contract of a kind, stating that after payment of six years of his life it shall revert to the said Pallehner to be disposed of freely by him. But what is that agreement worth now? Where are its guarantors? Dead, deposed, behind bars. Perhaps Pallehner's contract has been amended without his knowledge, perhaps it has been mislaid or even forgotten in the wreckage of all those millions of leaves. Don't you see? Can't you understand that you are caught up and spinning in the great wheel? Don't be deceived by the fatal illusion that the wheel is moving around you — you are moving with it.

"Everyone moves with it. The general secretary of the party has just been arrested. The wheel rolls back for him. The accuser becomes the accused, and so thoroughly accused that he may be in his grave before those against whom he had himself long since brought accusations have even been indicted. The wheel rolls back still farther, entrammeling the general secretary's associates and friends, perhaps his brother-in-law, conspirators against the state, all of them, and most of them happen to be Jews. Back six years to attend to a little unfinished business of the war, then, and Pallehner, who has not yet been arrested, is already clamoring for his release. For this is a peculiarity of the wheel and its interstices of time, in which all events are concurrent. Thus it is possible for a former minister of defense and member of the party presidium to take a parade in full ceremonial dress, acknowledging the ovations of the crowds from the balcony of honor, and to be a prisoner in Leopoldov at the same time.

"Sham and deceit, from top to bottom. Can such a government as this rule? With ministers who have to be bundled in and out of their cells for state occasions? The government does not rule. The party rules. Party and government are identical, for the members of one are members of the other. Concurrence of powers and concurrence of events: an inalienable property of the great wheel, a law of political physics! The Secretariat of the Central Committee of the Communist Party masquerades as the government and kills two birds with one stone; party business and government business, both are killed stone dead.

"But even these privileged holders of office, close to the hub of power, discover that they are not exempt from the vagaries of the wheel. The removal of Slansky makes plain how confident the Department of State Security has become. In fact it is not a department at all. It is not merely independent of the state and the party; it is already superordinate to them. That has been the change in these last few months.

"A suspicion in the corridors of the State Security headquarters is irreversibly a conviction in the courts. Security knows what nobody else knows. It cannot err, it cannot be seen to err, without jeopardizing its monopoly of information, and thus no one on whom it has laid its finger can be allowed to escape trial. This is the self-serving dynamism of the great wheel, its only certainty, its only claim to a kind of logic. The evidence is constructed and the confessions extorted to fit the case that Security has long since prepared against the accused. But the worst of it is: Security does not control the wheel either. It is carried by the same momentum as its victims. All that matters is that the wheel should never stop. So it rolls on and on and there is no end in sight, not for Tibor Lazar or Joseph Pallehner or for any of us. And you tell me you will be home in fifteen months!''

I never saw the face of Tibor Lazar. I never even tried to envisage it. I have only a memory of a voice and the words it improbably brought to me through a ventilation grid in my cell.

Were his predictions right? At least one of them was fulfilled within a week. I was taken from the infirmary and assigned to a transport of a hundred men that left Leopoldov early in the new year for an unknown destination.

The Road Builder

I<small>T</small> was snowing heavily on the morning the transport left Leopoldov. We stood shivering in the front court for over an hour. Snowflakes roosted on our caps, decorated threadbare shoulders with white epaulettes and raised mounds in memory of vanished boots. Where had they gone, those three and a half fortress years, through which my boots had walked me? Where were Oberle, Hoppe, Sellner, the priests and the Hungarian thieves? I knew none of the faces I saw in the yard. After six months in the infirmary my world was no longer familiar. Even the fortress itself seemed transfigured by the snow. I felt as if a cover had been drawn forever over the past.

And so I left Leopoldov at last. The men were divided into four groups and herded inside a length of chain, attached at either end to two handcuffed prisoners who walked at the front of each column. Armed guards and dogs followed. Curtains fell across the landscape. Soon there was no sign of Leopoldov behind us, the road in front had disappeared. Where were we going? Chained in our own moving enclosure we stumbled through the snow.

"Where are we going?"

Whenever a transport left the fortress the same fear gave the same answer: Siberia. We were being taken to Siberia.

The first leg of the journey to Siberia took two hours. We arrived at a deserted station. No sign of a train. The snow thickened. After half an hour we were marched a couple of hundred yards along the tracks to shelter in a cattle truck in a siding. The guards bolted the wagon and went away. They must have gone back to the station. We heard them whistling the dogs. We huddled in the cattle truck, wet and hungry, waiting for them to come back. But the guards didn't come back. They kept us waiting until nightfall.

I must have dozed off. A piercing sound, more like a shriek than a whistle, woke me to cold darkness. For a moment I thought the guards were whistling up the dogs, but of course it was a train. A train had arrived at the station. We could hear the hiss and clanging of the locomotive.

A minute later dogs barked and the guards began to shout. Bolts rattled and slammed, the door of the cattle truck thundered open, the sharp night air lunged in like a lash.

"Hop hop!"

The men tumbled stiffly out of the truck into the glare of a searchlight and the snapping jaws of the dogs. It seemed a long way down to the ground. I pitched headlong into the snow and sprained my wrist.

"Hop hop!"

We raced back along the tracks in single file, instinctively ducking our heads, as if anticipating a blow. Pain shot up my arm. I seemed to be running through bursts of mist, like the flares of a fire-eater, inexplicable, at first, for it had stopped snowing and the night was clear, until I realized it was the condensation of my own breath and the breath of the hundred panting men in whose slipstream I was running — a silvery-bluish slipstream, jets of air illuminating the night, and then steam, whiter, denser, clouds of smoke billowing from the funnel of the locomotive, black-plated and steel-pistoned, that suddenly loomed up in front of me.

"Last four cars! Hop hop hop!"

A line of guards, legs astride, flanked the platform. Baying dogs pranced and twisted on the leash. The smoke cleared. I ran on. It seemed to be a very long train, car after car, dark and silent; a goods train, perhaps. Lights at the end — four passenger cars had been tagged on. I was the last. I scrambled up the steps. A guard jumped onto the footplate behind me and shoved me into the corridor. The train began to move.

The car was a bare rectangular box — seats, racks, partitions, everything that could be dismantled had been taken out. Only the lamps, with curiously ornate shades, remained bracketed to the walls. It must once have been a dining car. We sprawled on the floorboards and had nothing to eat. I shut out the voices around me by putting my good ear to the floor, and listened to the rhythm of the wheels instead: where are we going, where are we going? They tossed the question back and forth, back and forth, I closed my eyes and instantly fell asleep.

When I awoke it was light. The wheels had acquired a different rhythm. I looked out of the window and saw an unbroken stream of whiteness. Most of the men were already awake. They crouched at the window and peered up at the sky. They were looking for the sun. A roof of cloud like a sheet of canvas left only a narrow tunnel between snow and sky through which the train could pass. It was light, the sun had come up, but as yet no indication of where. The men turned away from the window and began to grumble that they had not had anything to eat for twenty-four hours, but listening to the changed rhythm of the wheels I had completely lost my appetite. Why this haste? Ta-tá ta-tá, the flick of a rope, a double hitch — tying us to what? — coiled around the pale sun that emerged ahead of us in the eastern sky as the train slammed to a halt in Kaschau-Kosice, two hundred kilometers from the Soviet border.

We spent three days in Kosice. Apparently the transport had traveled the hundreds of kilometers from Leopoldov to eastern Slovakia as a result of some administrative error, but now that we were there our fate became casually dependent on administrative convenience: it might just be simpler to carry us over the border into the Russian vastness than to freight us all the way back to Bratislava or Prague. Kosice had inadequate facilities for a hundred unrequested prisoners, and almost no food. What to do? A provincial Slovak official, escorted by a major of the Russian army, walked down the line of a hundred men, prodding them with a greasy finger to test weight, muscle, and working condition. Large men with large appetites were not required in hungry, unemployed Slovakia, but much required by the Russian major, whose country, although no less hungry, was still suffering from a war deficit of twenty million pairs of working hands. About half the Leopoldov contingent, prodded out of further Slovakian responsibility by a nameless official that morning, disappeared that afternoon across the border into Soviet jurisdiction.

Did I regret the *Kasematten*, the pneumonia that had granted me the privilege of the infirmary's starvation rations? In the last six months I had lost a third of my weight. Fingers that cared to prod would encounter nothing but ribs and bones. I was a thin man, and thin men stayed in Kosice.

Convicts transferred from Leopoldov to the prison in Ilava normally reached their destination in a day, but it took our transport a week. Having survived the perilous detour to eastern Slovakia we found ourselves shunted a few hundred kilometers south to Debrecen in Hungary, and then west in the direction of Budapest. All this time we had no idea what our ultimate destination would be, and whether it might not still, so arbitrary was the route we traveled, turn out to be Siberia in the end. In the meantime we suffered from bitter cold and hunger. On some days we were given a bowl of the dour Russian gruel known as *kascha,* on other days nothing; sometimes there was water, sometimes not, and never any other form of heat than what our own bodies could generate. We took it in turns to crouch over a hole cut in the floor. An unforgettable railwayman in Hungary provided us with straw and a dozen blankets. How do forty men share a dozen blankets? On a journey like this, one made friends as passionately as one made enemies. People who had been mere strangers when we boarded the train in Leopoldov had become lifetime friends when we arrived in Ilava a week later, but none of those friendships survived except in my memory. That was one of the most disturbing aspects of prison life. What happened to Csaba, Boros, Welser? And what happened to the traveling companions who shared with me that odyssey from Leopoldov to Ilava? When we reached our destination they vanished from my life.

The prison of Ilava, like Leopoldov, shared no more of the neighboring village than its name. It stood isolated in the fields, surrounded by high walls, barbed wire, and turrets at regular intervals, which gave it more the appearance of a camp than a prison. The walls were high but not insuperable. Two convicts scaled them and escaped, encouragingly, on the day I arrived.

I was assigned to a team of builders. We lived and worked together for the next six months. Thirty architects, engineers, contractors and laborers shared a large room of about two hundred square meters, with a view on one side into the inner court and of the open sky on the other. If one stood on the table one could see the fields beyond the prison wall.

About a third of the inmates were pre-1948 politicals like myself; the remainder had been imprisoned by the Communists after the February coup on charges of sabotage. There were only two criminals, both of them murderers.

Sabotage meant the embezzlement of funds or building materials, usually cement, by men in commissarial charge of companies they had previously owned. Quitt, whose accounts I had polished in Leopoldov, was a typical example of this new generation of saboteurs. The inmates of our room had between them scored a total of two hundred and fifty years for cement manipulation alone.

Our straw pallets were laid out on iron bedsteads, side by side, as they had been in Leopoldov. My neighbor on the left was a German, a V-2 missile engineer by the name of Silversdorf, who had been charged with contributing to the development of "inhuman weapons" and sentenced to ten years.

Silversdorf was the builders' team's "inventor." Lack of materials meant that a lot of on-site equipment had to be improvised, and Silversdorf was very good at this. He had a highly ingenious and rather childlike mind.

The pallet on the other side was occupied by Mansovic. Mansovic was a murderer. He had strangled his own child.

Before he was sent to prison Mansovic had been a builder's laborer with a wife and large family. Conversations with all kinds of criminals in the course of my prison career had nourished in me the opinion that although intelligence was not necessarily an ally of conscience, stupidity was its declared enemy — stupidity seemed to anesthetize whatever was wakeful in a man, including his conscience. Mansovic had killed his child because he already had too many. The court might still have found grounds for compassion had it not been for the way in which Mansovic murdered his child and the way he justified his crime.

He had carried the infant out of the house one morning without telling his wife, throttled it and thrown the bundle into the river. Why had he thrown it into the river? Because the body had to be disposed of, and the bridge was a convenient spot where he also occasionally disposed of cats. Mansovic did not regard what he had done as a crime, and however much we explained to him that it was a crime we were unable to change his opinion.

"It was my child," he repeated stonily.

"What d'you mean, your child?"

"It was *mine*. It belonged to me. It was my child."

"That doesn't mean you could kill it."

"If it belongs to me I can do what I like with it."

He wouldn't budge. He couldn't budge. What we tried to explain to him was beyond his comprehension.

"Did you kill the child because it was your own, or because you already had too many children to feed? Would you kill a child *just* because it was your own?"

Mansovic shook his head. He didn't understand. What was the fuss about? Why didn't *we* understand?

One day he had an idea. He took off one of his boots. He turned the boot over in his hands and held it up.

"This is a boot. See? It's my boot."

I nodded.

"My boot. I can do whatever I like with it."

He got up. Everyone was watching him.

Mansovic walked over to the stove in the middle of the room and threw the boot into the fire.

After that we gave up our efforts to convince Mansovic. He didn't understand the different meanings of own boot and own child. I don't think Mansovic was evil. His stupidity was evil. The sacrifice of his boot even showed a queer kind of willingness. He sacrificed his boot to his stupidity, just as he had his child. And the boot was a considerable sacrifice. There was no replacement. For the next few months he hobbled about in odd footwear. Mansovic's feet must have spent an uncomfortable winter.

During the slack season when the ground was frozen no new foundations could be laid, but we had plenty of work indoors. In the previous autumn the prison builders had erected a block of apartments for the warders and their families on a site halfway between the prison and the village. Throughout February and March we worked on the plumbing, wiring, plastering and decorating so that the apartments would be ready for the warders in the spring.

Making use of prison labor to build accommodation for prison staff had been an ill-advised undertaking from the start. I thought it looked rather a handsome building, but the architect who had designed it gave me a confidential guarantee that within seven years it would either fall down of its own accord or have to be demolished. Long before then he would have been released and returned to his own country. With some pride he told me he had made such a good job of building it badly that the state inspectors he escorted around the site had overlooked his furtive handiwork and given the project their official blessing. More obvious cases of sabotage, although usually unattributable, had already delayed completion of the building by a year.

Now, however, the walls stood — at least for the time being.

The architect's sulfurous torch of technical wizardry and schoolboy prank was handed on to Silversdorf. It was the kind of thing at which Silversdorf excelled. The prison administration unwarily approved his appointment as chief electrician.

Silversdorf had spent his war years wiring up missiles that would fly hundreds of miles to bomb enemy cities. It was this man who was now encharged with wiring up the warders' new housing block. Work proceeded smoothly. Silversdorf laid his cables and threaded his wires, Mansovic plastered over the walls and I painted them white. We worked overtime and were paid premium rates. Prison supervisors visiting the site congratulated the team on the rapid progress.

One curiosity about the apartments that I noticed when I began painting them was the lack of storage space in the kitchens. There were no larders. I asked the architect if denying larders to the future occupants was another detail in his malicious design, but apparently he had only been complying with the new building regulations. It was all part of a Communist drive to reallocate the consumption of food in privacy to doctrinally more salubrious state canteens; the digestive should be incorporated into the socialist system, into the larger body politic. But this attempt to socialize food did not succeed. It only encouraged people to install shelves. The hoarding of food appeared to be an irrepressible human activity.

The warders' larderless housing was completed punctually by the end of April. Local dignitaries and party officials invited from Bratislava attended the opening ceremony. The prison director made a speech on the useful employment of convict labor. A band played. Members of the builders' team, although not actually invited, were rewarded with a basket of savory meat pies. The party officials returned to Bratislava, the warders and their families moved into their new home.

At some time in the evening it exploded and caught fire. The fire was put out. There were no injuries, but extensive damage had been caused. The warders and their families moved back into the village on the following day.

A commission of enquiry later established that at least nine detonations had occurred throughout the building during the peak-load hours of the evening. The explosions had been localized and staggered by means of a sophisticated time switch that the commission's civilian electricians had never seen before. Obviously the building had been booby-trapped. No injuries, but nonetheless an extremely dangerous act of sabotage. Where was Silversdorf?

Silversdorf was eating the last of the savory meat pies. Apologetic but not contrite, he disclaimed all knowledge of the matter. He must have made a mistake somewhere. Was that his fault? It was the first time he had turned his hand to a job of this kind. But nobody believed his excuses. All privileges of the pampered builders' team were suspended at once and Silversdorf was sentenced to six months' solitary confinement.

Another consequence of the Silversdorf escapade was the breaking up of our professional community just at the moment when we were beginning to feel integrated. The prison administration detected a conspiracy of which Silversdorf was the volcanic furuncle. The conspirators had to be disbanded. Thus I found myself loaned out to the prison in Rosenberg as a casual laborer.

The town of Rosenberg lay at the foot of the Tatra Mountains, with magnificent scenic views of completely unspoiled countryside. I arrived there in the summer of 1952, pregnant with the seed of a great hope that the sight of these broader horizons nurtured impatiently inside me: the life-giving hope of freedom, in nine months my deliverance! New horizons, the fresh air of the mountains! Space and air! I coasted through those early summer days, digging trenches, replacing bars, restoring walls for my successors to be confined in, and thought with cruel jubilation: not for me! Not for me!

Not for me the hooks that I helped to mortar into the walls of the cellars of Rosenberg Prison, not for me — for whom then, those sinister hooks that borrowed the resemblance to a slaughterhouse? Resemblance? The meat that would soon hang upside down from these hooks would still be alive, that was the difference. Flayed until the confessions had been bled from the flesh, but still alive! Dumb country animals, local peasants who had blundered into a futile uprising to liberate their imprisoned priests, but not dumb for long — they were the talking carcasses to be hoisted onto the hooks. Could I have been expected to know that at the time? Should I have guessed, when the builders were sent down to convert the cellars into a cold storage room? The job was done by a gang of casual laborers brought in from outside. I was one of them: a casual laborer. My heart was not in the job, no. My heart strained for its own survival.

Not for me the juveniles' prison where I worked briefly as a bricklayer, for I was not a youthful prisoner whose life still lay immured ahead of him, I had already done my time. Life? For some of them it would be finished, life of any kind, before I had resumed mine. It was a small prison, for it had little to accommodate, a clutch of boys, mere shreds of lives, aged between twelve and eighteen.

Two of them had been sentenced, they were old enough for that, to death, but at seventeen they were not old enough for that — and in that hiatus between sentence and death, which by law was the privilege of their eighteenth birthdays, the juveniles' prison granted them a seven-month space to catch their breath — for what? For a final exhalation, extinction, snuffing out. They were waiting, they were *maturing,* until ripe for execution. What had they done? They had carried messages between life and death, dodging back and forth across the border between Vienna and Bratislava as agents of an imperialist power.

No, not for me. Rosenberg was not for me. The broader horizons, the space and air of the early summer shrank back into the narrow courtyard of that prison. How could it be in my heart to wait impatiently for time to pass? Pregnant with hopes for what? My hopes succumbed to a morning sickness and clouded over; premature, stillborn.

At the time of the peasants' uprising on behalf of their imprisoned priests Bibles were once again released for distribution in the cells of Rosenberg Prison. And one imperialist power, while hanging the childish agents of the other, sent its own agents into the prisons to recruit mercenaries for a war of which they had never heard on the other side of the world. Hardly ensconced in their scriptural corners, the Bible readers were again dragged out and permitted to attend evening seminars on Marxist-Leninist teachings instead. Our smaller world, which we thought we knew, was inheriting the confusion of the larger world, about which we could only guess. Even the hard and fast distinction between captivity and freedom buckled under this uncertainty. Only one thing was certain — physical toil, the body's day-to-day fatigue and the mind's forgetful sleep.

What could have been better at such a time than to work

in the forests at the foot of the mountains? Shirtsleeved into summer mornings, boots crunching on cobbled streets, each day a reassuring encounter with the town's unchanging routine, of which we ourselves became a part — what could have been better than this? The local people soon grew used to the gangs of navvies marching through the streets. We could imagine ourselves, almost, to be ordinary folk.

"There she goes!"

And there she went, punctually at eight o'clock each morning, the office girl with the auburn hair and spruce white shoes. She passed us on the other side of the street as we waited at the gates of the timber yard. A real live woman. The convicts' eyes followed her in a swarm, loosening her shoulder bag, drawing the blouse back from her shoulders and the skirt down over her hips, and before she turned the corner she would have wriggled out of a dozen shades of underwear into the emperor's suit of clothes, naked from her auburn collar down to her chaste white shoes.

"Now — now — look at that! Oh ho!"

The men laughed and cheered. Every morning it was the same.

How could I have expected my brother-in-law Karol to recognize me among that raucous crowd of men in their blue-gray uniforms and with their shorn heads? I saw him one morning through the windscreen of a large black car that was waiting while the convicts crossed the street. It was ten years since our last meeting at a reception in Bratislava. He was a Communist even then, and in the meantime he had been appointed rector of the university in recognition of his loyalty to the cause. An eminent man, my brother-in-law! Something must have caught his attention. Perhaps I gave a start. He stared at me. Involuntarily I began to raise my hand in a motion of greeting, which for some reason I never completed. Not just the gulf of ten years, but another distance there had always been between us. Did he recognize me in that encounter of a few seconds? If he did he gave no sign of it. Perhaps there was nothing left for him to recognize, not even as the observance of mere formality. Perhaps I had sunk beneath the necessity for such a gesture. This thought stayed uneasily with me long after the black car had driven on.

Barking fallen timber on the forest slopes I thought of my brother-in-law, an important man in his large black car, busy with the administration of his university, and found to my surprise that I did not envy him. I thought of another man I had known in the past, a leader of the Pressburg business community before the war, greedy for honors, wealth, power, and I did not regret his passing. I did not envy my former self either. I thought of nothing beyond the end of the log I straddled with my two-handed blade, peeling spruce bark in stark white strips through the unending forest of that summer, as if in all the world there were nothing else I could have done.

It was at this point in my life that I met a man who was known to the convicts as the road builder. Nobody knew the road builder's name. He said he no longer needed a name. He was German, they knew that much. They thought he'd gone a bit funny in the head.

We passed him every morning on our way through the forest where he spent the summer resurfacing the track that wound down the mountain to the timber yard in the valley. He worked alone, a long, lean, tattered figure in the ruins of a fur hat. The convicts made fun of this bizarre scarecrow of a man.

"Hey, road builder! What happened to your name? Did you leave it behind in Siberia?"

"Ah."

The road builder leaned against the shaft of his shovel and smiled good-naturedly.

"When are you going home, road builder?"

"When God wills," he replied easily.

"When God wills! And what weather does he will us?"

"The weather will keep."

The road builder was always right about the weather. He said he could tell it in his bones.

The convicts worked their way down through the forest from the ridge of the mountain toward the valley. The road builder worked his way up. Day by day we drew closer. Sometimes I heard the chink of his pickax and the barking rattle of gravel on his shovel. Sometimes the road meandered away into a gully and I lost the sound of him altogether. The sound of the road builder at work was the accompaniment of the mountain. He merged with the sounds that had been scored for it by nature, the wind and the streams and the drowsy murmuring among the flowers. He was part of its silence, too.

Summer sank into autumn and spread ripples of sunlight over a softer mountain. The first mists stole up out of the valley. A hazy afternoon light rang through the forest like a muted bell. The days became shorter, the air moister. In early October a swirling fog closed on the mountain, transfiguring the shrouded trees into a ghostly fleet of ships, becalmed with furled masts. From time to time the shouts of men and the splintering of timber bodied out of the surrounding silence. The fog rolled down the slopes and poured into the gullies, rebounding in dense vaporous plumes. In an enchanted forest stumps could uproot themselves and take on living forms, huge boulders were transformed into lurking trolls. And other things moved, outside my imagination. I could not see them, but I heard the steady pounding of their feet, or at least stamping of a kind, which is what it was. For when the fog suddenly lifted one morning I found myself beside a track in a clearing and saw the road builder pounding the earth with a weighted iron bar.

"Good morning."

"Ah. The fog has lifted . . ."

The road builder stopped his pounding and walked on slowly to the edge of the clearing, inspecting the track.

At noon the sun came out. The road builder and I sat on a log eating our lunches. From time to time the undergrowth around us crackled as the trees shed their moisture in a flurry of raindrops. The road builder cocked his head, as if listening to the mountain.

"I know this mountain," he said. "Three years I've been here now."

"And before that?"

"Before that there was the road."

When he had finished his lunch the road builder told me his story.

"I was a soldier once. Even then I moved earth. I was a sapper. I joined the troops garrisoned in Prague, and then I went to Russia. I was one of the first prisoners to be taken. They put the prisoners to work in Siberia. Somehow I got separated from the other prisoners. For days I waited on a bench at a station in a village so remote that the train stopped for passengers only once a week. I had been told to wait for the next train. But one night the captain of the local militia came to the station, accompanied by an old man who spoke German, and ordered me to go with him into the village. This captain treated me kindly, but he was a crazy fellow. Throughout the night we sat in his room drinking vodka, and when morning came the old man and I were so drunk that we could hardly walk to the door. The captain jumped up and ran out into the village to fetch a horse and cart. He bundled us into the back of the cart,

took the reins, and set off at a cracking pace. I heard a
train whistle, and I thought he must be in such a hurry
because he wanted to get me back to the station in time,
but he drove off in the opposite direction. He drove through
the village and straight out into the tundra.

"That brisk ride through the sharp morning air brought
me back to my senses. When the captain reined in I was
stone sober. The sun was climbing into a cloudless sky.
Land and sky met at the horizon. One could have turned
them upside down, it would have made no difference. The
level wastes of the steppe stretched for miles and miles
without a single tree or shrub.

"The captain leaped down from the cart and strode off
into the tundra. The old man and I stumbled after him as
best we could. The captain laughed and joked. He was in
high spirits. He told me that the government planned to
build a factory here, and when the factory had been completed a town would be built, a town for thousands of
people in the middle of the tundra. A splendid town! He
had seen the plans himself. They had even made a start on
the project, yes, work was already in progress, but it had
not yet got very far. He wanted us to see the site. It wasn't
much of a site, he said, but nonetheless, a beginning, a
brave beginning! The captain talked and talked and after
we had walked for a while we came to a river.

"A bridge had been built over the river. It was an im-
pressive bridge, secured on huge concrete piles and broad
enough for two-way traffic. But it led nowhere. It did no
more than span the river, beginning on one side and ending
on the other. But then what more than that could one ask
of a bridge, said the captain. Later it would lead somewhere — to the village, for a start. All the bridge needed
was a road.

"As we walked back to the cart the captain made me a

proposal. I had been captured by the Russians and become a prisoner of war. They would feed and clothe me, and in return I would have to work. He wanted me to build the first section of road across the tundra. It might take two years, or it might take four — that would depend on me. When I had finished the road I would be free.

"What alternative did I have? The alternative was a labor camp. If I refused to build the road here I would find myself building another somewhere else, or perhaps worse, be put to work in the mines. We had heard bad stories about the labor camps in Russia. And as for their side of the bargain, well, I had no faith in that. A prisoner of war remained a prisoner only as long as there was a war. I would go home when the war ended, whether I had finished their road or not.

"I agreed to the captain's proposal. The next day I began to build the road. I went out into the tundra with a wheelbarrow, pickax, shovel and hoe. It was August 1941.

"These were my only tools. I had no surveying instruments, no machines and no human help. I would build the road alone. God would help me.

"I set to work immediately. I was young and strong. In a few weeks I had driven hundreds of posts into the ground in a straight line from the village to the bridge over the river. The land was as flat as a board. The road metal, sand and gravel needed for the foundation of a road had been brought in by rail when the bridge was built and had been lying in the station depot ever since. The Russians supplied me with a horse and cart to transport the materials from the depot to the road construction site in the tundra. I had to shovel everything into the cart by hand.

"I did not realize how soon the winter came to the northern steppe and how long it stayed. Winter was not a season there. It was a state of siege. For six months the village was engulfed in snow and ice. The posts marking the road disappeared under the white drifts of the tundra. In winter the tundra came alive. It roared and snarled like a wild animal.

"Sometimes I was put to work unloading supplies at the depot. I swept snow from the roofs. I mended tools. I was quartered at the militia post, free to come and go as I pleased. How could I have escaped? I was a prisoner of the tundra like the rest of the inhabitants. They were friendly people. I learned Russian and could talk with them in their own language. I drank with them. Sometimes the serving girl at the inn would let me through a back door at night and we shared our warmth in her bed. But for most of the winter I waited. I waited, and thought of the road.

"Four years passed. My strength did not ebb. God was with me.

"One morning in the spring of 1945 I hitched my horse to the cart and drove to the station depot. People were running in and out of their houses and talking excitedly in the street. They told me the fascist armies had been defeated. The war had ended. I turned the horse around and drove back to the militia post. The captain of the militia who had fetched me from the station and set me to work on the road four years ago had been drafted to the front soon after. He was replaced by a cripple, a youthful veteran with one leg. I applied to this man for the official authorization of my release. The war had ended. I was entitled to go home.

"The new captain told me it was not as easy as that. There were hundreds of thousands of German prisoners of war interned in Russian camps. It would be a long time before all these men could be sent home. I would have to wait my turn. He would notify me when my discharge papers arrived.

"My papers arrived two months later, but they said nothing about my discharge. The captain explained that prisoners working on assignments that the authorities classed as war reparations projects could not be sent home until those projects had been completed. I would have to stay until I had built the road.

"I walked through the village with an empty heart. Streamers decorated the houses, a band was playing in the street. I walked out to the tundra. My heart was on a level there. The wind blowing across the empty steppe blew straight into my heart. It blew through me. My body offered no resistance. The steppe and I were the same emptiness. All day I sat at the end of the road and gazed across the intervening space. Less than half of the road had been built.

"I began working again. I don't know when, I made no decision. There is a gap in my memory. The road had become a habit. I went on working out of habit. Perhaps that was the only way over to the river on the other side. It was hard to begin once I had stopped. It was easy to go on once I had begun. The road grew out of itself. It seemed to grow of its own accord. I looked down my arm and watched the road grow out of my hand. It became an extension of myself. Sometimes it seemed I was no longer building the road. Sometimes it seemed the road was building me.

"On white summer nights when the sun skimmed the horizon and bordered the blue tundra with a rim of gold I watched the road catch the first spark of the light that was neither day nor night and begin to glow. It glowed up out of the surrounding wastes and floated across the dark, a white causeway suspended in the dark. It ran over the river into the morning horizon. The road stretched right across the tundra.

"I surfaced the road with broken-stone ballast. I hitched

the horse to a railway sleeper and ploughed the road for a whole summer. I ploughed through the evening into the morning and slept for a few hours at noon. I ploughed my life into the surface of the road. I hardly slept in summer. I shared the rhythm of the road. When the road disappeared in winter I felt my own life ebb in me. I went out like a tide. I slept for days and nights.

"At the end of one summer I finished the road. It was a good road, smooth and firm. I could walk on it barefoot from the village to the river and back again without cutting my feet. Every stone in it, every grain of sand, had been put there with my own hands.

"It had taken eight years to build the road.

"I went to the captain of the militia and asked for my discharge papers.

"On the night before my departure I walked out into the tundra for the last time. It was a starlit night. The steppe was dead. There was no moon. But the road was shining. It drove a shaft through the night. I knelt on the road and wept.

"I carried the shining with me on my journey back to the West. Nothing could dim it. When I reached the Czechoslovakian frontier the border guards saw from my papers that I had once belonged to a German division garrisoned in Prague. I was sentenced to prison for five years and brought to Rosenberg. That is why I am here now. That is my story."

The road builder got up from the log on which we were sitting and walked down to the track. I sat in silence for a few minutes.

"So you have two more years to serve?" I asked, for want of something better to say.

"Two years, God willing."

God willing! How naturally the phrase came to his lips! How mysteriously! But I believed him when he said it.

"You are a mystic, you know."

"I am a road builder," he replied.

"And where do you come from?"

"I come from an island in the North Sea."

He picked up his shovel and began to walk up the track.

"And will you be going back to your island?" I called after him.

The road builder gave no answer. Perhaps he hadn't heard.

By the end of October the convicts had worked their way down to the valley. We no longer met the road builder on our way to work in the mornings. When our assignment came to an end a week later he was still up there somewhere on the mountain.

I returned to the prison in Ilava at the beginning of winter. In another four months I would have served my sentence. Almost six years had passed. Four more months and I would be a free man.

Kunzendorf

ARLY in March, a few days before I was due to be
released, news reached Ilava that Stalin had died.
Rumors at once flared up in the prison. An amnesty, there
would be an amnesty for all political prisoners! On the
following day we heard the drone of aircraft; someone reported that they had been identified positively as American
planes. Eisenhower was sending in troops, Czechoslovakia
had been invaded! Amnestied by the Russians or liberated
by the Americans? The spark of hope exploded into hys-
teria. But even during these feverish days of speculation
the bickering continued over a very much more modest
prize: who should have the privilege of the bed under the
window when its present occupant left Ilava?

A couple of months before my departure the mere prospect of freedom had begun to segregate me from the other
inmates. I could no longer share their hopes, for I had no
need of them now. I had certainty, an unshakeable certainty
for myself alone. The intensity of the prisoner's longings,
tautened by the very remoteness of their fulfillment, like
the desire for a meal or for a woman or a sheet to lie on
at night, began to slacken in me from the moment fulfillment became the closer reality. Impending fact punctured
the bubble of imagination. An unaccountable, bounding

urge of joy, accountable at last, suddenly went lame. Now that I could reach out and clasp the grail I found myself wondering what I should do with it.

I was not spared the jibes of my fellow prisoners.

"Ah well, it's different for Joseph, now."

"He won't want to have anything to do with the likes of us."

They wished me well, and they meant it, but what could have been more natural than their envy? What could have been truer to prison life than to start arguing over my bed even before I had vacated it?

On the morning of the fourteenth of March I reported to the guardroom by the prison gates. I waited there for a couple of hours.

Shortly after noon the door opened and a young guard carrying a briefcase stepped in.

"Joseph Pallehner?"

"Yes."

"Taken into custody on the fourteenth of March, 1947?"

"Yes."

"Six years?"

"Yes."

"You will accompany me to the station."

The guard handed a piece of paper to the duty officer, who signed and returned it. A sentry unlocked the smaller door in the main gate and I followed the guard outside.

We walked through the village to Ilava station. It was an overcast, windless day. The guard never said a word.

I stood on the platform and looked down the line. For some reason I started counting the sleepers, but at the end of the platform they vanished into perspective and soon I had lost count. Somewhere in the distance the railway track reached a border, and on the other side of the border my family would be waiting for me. I walked down the platform toward the border. My heart began to beat a little faster. Still no sign of the train that was supposed to take me there. I reached the end of the platform and reluctantly turned back. I walked up and down impatiently several times.

"It won't get you there any quicker," remarked the guard. He tossed the butt of his cigarette onto the platform and ground it with his heel.

"And anyway, what's the hurry?"

I looked at him in astonishment.

"Hurry? Don't you realize that today I shall be at home with my family? After six years in prison —"

"Home?" echoed the guard. "But you're not going home."

I didn't understand what he was saying.

"You're not going home," repeated the guard. "What gave you that idea? Nobody ever gets sent back to the West, not even prisoners who've done their time. Didn't you know?"

I reeled.

"They don't get sent back? Then where are they sent?"

"I'm not allowed to say."

My head swam. What had the guard said? I asked him to repeat it, but my words were lost in the thunderous motion of the train pulling into the station. The guard opened a door and told me to get in. I climbed numbly up into the carriage.

I sat at the window and looked blindly out. For several minutes I could see and hear nothing. Not the journey home, not sent back, never. I felt the train gathering speed. It was rushing into nowhere. My God! I closed my eyes. I didn't want to see. They could take me where they would. I ceased to care. Flashes jumbled in my head, too brief to make up an image. Then I heard the long, mournful shriek of the train whistle and opened my eyes. The guard had gone. Everything had gone. I was swaddled in darkness.

Of course I couldn't see. The train had entered a tunnel.

On the other side of the darkness the train came out of the tunnel. We were going somewhere after all, whether I wanted to or not. My curiosity got the better of me. I looked out of the window. I knew where we were. We were traveling north. I had made this journey many times in my life. And sure enough, after a short while the train arrived at Sillein.

We waited in Sillein for about ten minutes. The locomotive let off steam while part of the train was uncoupled. The platform was deserted. I listened to the slow hiss of the train and an indistinct, rhythmic pounding. Which way from Sillein? We could turn west through Moravia. Or we could turn east to Poland. The hiss faded, the pounding ceased. Silence. The points had already been set. I heard a whistle. The carriage gave a jerk and rolled forward.

My heart seized up.

The train snaked through the points.

It reached a clear stretch and gathered speed. We remained south of the border. We were traveling west.

Had the guard played a cruel trick? Dare I hope for even more, greedy again, now that the worst had been averted? And how much of this uncertainty could a man take?

Somewhere between my still hoping and not yet daring to hope again the train halted at an interim destination. We got out at Mährisch-Ostrau, close to the Polish border.

A jeep was waiting in front of the station. We climbed into the jeep, drove through the town and out into the country. After a while we turned off the main road and drove into a wood.

I was ready for anything. Anything might happen. Perhaps it was true that prisoners who had served their sentence were never sent back, or sent anywhere, for that matter. Perhaps they were taken into a wood and shot.

In the middle of the wood we reached a fence. Behind the fence lay a compound, a camp of a kind. The camp had no ditches, as far as I could see, no turrets or barbed wire, and the gates stood open. There didn't seem to be any sentries either. We drove straight in.

The jeep stopped outside a hut at the camp entrance. The guard who had escorted me from Ilava knocked on a door marked *Lagerkommandant* and went into the hut. He told me to wait outside. While I waited I took stock of my surroundings. The compound was made up of fifteen to twenty wooden huts, or barracks, enclosed by a wire fence. That was all. I could see someone on the other side of the compound, hanging up washing on a line between two barracks. I realized to my surprise that it was a woman. I felt immensely grateful to this unknown woman just for being there at that particular time, for I knew that as long as I remained in a place where a woman could hang up washing I would not be shot, for the time being I was safe.

After a while the guard emerged from the hut and told me the *Kommandant* wanted to have a word with me. The guard got back into the jeep and drove off. I went into the hut.

A large, bald man of about fifty was sitting at a desk with a file open in front of him. He greeted me in German.

"Just a few words about the camp regulations," he said briskly. "There are about two hundred people detained here, all of them German. I say people detained rather than prisoners because you are allowed a measure of freedom here. From eight in the morning until eight in the evening the gates are open, and you may come and go as you please. You are required to work. A suitable occupation will be found for you. Life is not so bad at all here. However —"

He got up and walked around the desk to the window.

"A word of warning. The curfew must be observed. After years in prison many men find the attractions of the local village irresistible. They sniff freedom. They can walk out without guards. There is plenty of food. Drink. And of course there are women. . . .There are lots of reasons why a man can forget the evening curfew, and occasionally some men do. You will meet them in the village. They no longer have any of the obligations imposed on inmates of the camp, but they have also forfeited their rights. Anyone who fails to return to the camp by curfew places himself outside its jurisdiction and is regarded as having opted to become a citizen of this country. His status as an alien prisoner is no longer recognized, and he thereby forfeits the right of repatriation. Forever. Only inmates of the camp can expect to be sent home. Is that clear?"

I nodded.

"Any questions?"

"Yes. You said inmates of the camp can expect to be sent home. But when? How long am I going to be detained here?"

"Indefinitely."

My heart sank.

"It depends on political developments. And that can take time. Some people have been waiting in this camp for a couple of years. Well . . . you can pick up your bedding from the storeroom opposite," he pointed through the window, "over there. I've assigned you to Hut Fifteen."

"Isn't there any other hut available?"

"Any other hut?"

"I'm superstitious about that number."

"Oh. I'll see what I can do."

I left the *Lagerkommandant* at his desk and took a stroll around the compound. Then I walked around it a second time — outside the fence, just to get the feel. But all I felt was weariness. Released from prison, but not yet free; a taunting measure of freedom, enough to whet my appetite, not enough to still my hunger.

The following day black flags hung unfurled in the village street, a token of official mourning for the president of the republic, Klement Gottwald, who had died on March the fourteenth. I had been tried and imprisoned in Gottwald's name, both of us, in our different ways, had served our time and both of us, had law been right, were due for release on the same day. Gottwald got his, but I didn't get mine. He made me a private legacy by which I would always remember him. And so I began the seventh year of captivity, captivity with a measure of freedom, enough to get the measure of captivity, which called itself Kunzendorf.

In Kunzendorf, a kind of no-man's-land where official time stood still, enabling prisoners to continue serving sentences that by any other count were over, I anticipated the future with memories of the past. On the day of my arrival I was confronted with the anniversary of my departure, with a canvas bag my wife had packed for me in 1947: a bag of memories. It was handed to me by the clerk in the storeroom where I went to receive my bedding. In the course of the years the canvas had become brittle, the color had long since faded, and when the clerk opened the bag it released a cold, stale smell. With wrinkled nose he removed the meager exhibits and placed them on the counter. Rag identifiable as shirt. Rag identifiable as singlet. A key-ring with three keys. A notebook, the leaves corrugated and swollen, protruding from the binding like a tongue from the mouth of a corpse. Fragments of photographs of children, shrunken portraits long since outgrown by their subjects. Leather wallet containing two hundred and eighty-three reichsmark (withdrawn from currency five years previously). A wristwatch. And a wedding ring. Would I please sign a receipt for my property?

I carried the bag to Hut 18, three doors down from superstition. I emptied the contents of the bag onto the table and looked at them reluctantly. These things were no more mine than they were the clerk's who had wrinkled his nose. The garments had disintegrated, the notebook was indecipherable and the money worthless. I threw them away with the bag. I wound up the watch. It had stopped for six years, but it still worked. The wedding ring slipped off my finger. It had been worn by a fleshy man. I would wear it on my middle finger instead.

I felt like a scavenger, rifling the pockets of a dead man.

This feeling persisted for a long time. In Kunzendorf I had a measure of freedom to explore an identity that had long been extinguished. The convict's shorn head was again allowed its natural hair, he exchanged prison garb for civilian clothes, a number for the individuality of a name. But he could not simply be restored to these things, reassuming possession of what was rightfully his as if nothing had intervened but the expropriation of years. The sensation of hair growing unimpeded on my head was as unfamiliar as the thoughts that began to unfold inside it. I had thrown money away, worthless perhaps, but I had done so without any regret. The businessman would immediately have converted that sum of money into the new currency in order to be able to put a figure to his loss. Somewhere between Pilsen and Kunzendorf the businessman in me had died. I had difficulty with conversions of any kind. I continued to eat furtively in corners, I would forget to wipe myself when I had been to the lavatory, I waited instinctively for orders at open gates. I retained the murky, slavish habits a dispossessed humanity acquires to survive. I felt like debased coinage myself. The past was no help. Only the future could reform me.

My sister-in-law in Pressburg sent me a suit. She had it made to measure the tailor's dummy that she had retrieved from my villa at the end of the war and kept ever since. But the suit didn't fit. It was much too large.

Nothing fitted.

In the first few weeks I noticed little change in myself. Officially I was not a convict, unofficially I continued to labor like one, not breaking rocks, but shoveling glowing ash onto the slag heaps of the local foundry. It was strenuous work, the hardest assignment in Kunzendorf, and it was reserved for the uncomplaining newcomers. I worked there with Willy Hartmann, whom I had got to know on the original transport from Dachau to Pilsen in 1947. Willy had spent the intervening years in Brünn, and he had weathered them better than most. All day we pushed wagons from the foundry yard to the dump, knocked the bolts from the doors and shoveled out the slag. They were old-fashioned wagons that couldn't be tipped. Everything had to be done by hand. Willy once tried to make the work easier by laying a board on top of the slag so that he could shovel it down, but the board sank under his weight into the smoldering ash and began to burn. I pulled him out with my shovel. He was lucky not to have been roasted alive.

After we had shoveled our statutory month of slag at the foundry Willy and I graduated to a more comfortable job as interior decorators in a housing block for the employees of the iron works at Mährisch-Ostrau. I lay on scaffolding with a bandage over my eyes and whitewashed ceilings, half the time I lay there and did nothing. Willy saw to it that we were undisturbed. He put out a Wet Paint sign and boarded up the entrance.

For most of the time I talked to Willy I was addressing not him but the ceiling, either the ceiling I could reach out and paint during the day or the ceiling I could reach out and touch at night. We lived in the same hut. The bunks were arranged in tiers of three, with Willy in the middle and myself on top. This good-natured man had a robust soul and the constitution of a horse, absorbing the shocks of his prison years without apparent ill effect, and an equally vigorous digestive system that vaporized food with the same promptness. He was particularly fond of garlic and beans. Thus the remarks that reached me on the rebound from the ceiling carried Willy's unmistakable flavor, a highly distinctive personal smell compounded of warm garlic and discreetly broken wind, slyly chiding my nostrils by way of broaching my drowsy mind.

"Are you awake, Joseph?"

Ouf. For a man who was hard of hearing perhaps it was just as well.

Our hut could accommodate fifteen persons, and on some nights, with a little squeezing, it found room for a sixteenth. Tschubla tiptoed into the hut when most of the men were asleep and usually left before they woke. Tschubla shared the bottom berth by the door with a colonel who was the senior resident of the camp. They were narrow bunks, not intended for two, and a creaking tête-à-tête with the colonel sometimes spilled thunderously onto the floor.

Tschubla was a woman. Formerly a landowner in Silesia, she had somehow got entrammeled in the machinery of the war. I never learned what fate had brought her to Kunzendorf. She was one of six female inmates who shared the camp with two hundred men.

Two of the Kunzendorf women had belonged to a field communications unit, two were nurses, and one had done propaganda work. They were all in their thirties with the exception of Tschubla, who was over fifty, and all of them had found it preferable to form an attachment rather than to be plundered as free booty among two hundred men and their sometimes rapacious overseers. So Tschubla became the colonel's attachment. The men respected that. We knew that outside Kunzendorf they both had another marriage, but that did not concern us. Nobody wanted brawls over the women. Attachments settled the question.

The women lived in a hut of their own, which by common consent was out of bounds for all male inmates, including attachments. At night the women carried their favors into the men's quarters, in exchange for the benefits of protection and perhaps also for their own pleasure. Their only privacy was the dark. I wondered why Tschubla preferred a dark bristling with fifteen invisible men, even snoring men, to a dark gracefully interspersed with half a dozen similarly occupied women. I tackled the colonel on this delicate issue and was given a surprisingly bluff answer. The women were jealous of one another, he said. Given the alternative, they performed more willingly in the presence of other men than in the presence of other women.

In their poor sense of comradeship the Kunzendorf women reminded me of Leopoldov's priests. There was nothing priestlike about the women, but I realized why I had felt there was something womanish about the priests. They had in common the same caviling tone with one another, the same brittle solidarity that broke up as soon as personal interests were threatened. Outside their sexual appetites the men seemed able to satisfy all the urges of human companionship, shelter, mutual reliance, and even gentleness, within their own kind, but the women did not form such friendships. They turned to men for what their own sex was unable to supply. Thus the women's need of their men became much greater than the men's need of women.

There was nothing furtive or shameful about the women's nocturnal visits. They were as natural a part of life in Kunzendorf as the toilet facilities, where the women squatted thigh by thigh with their fellow male inmates. Without exception the partners remained loyal to their attachment. In some cases the attachment survived beyond the provisional understanding on which it had been formed and continued, with unhappy consequences, to flourish in the free world outside Kunzendorf, where it found itself subject to other constraints, the claims of other partners.

One hundred and ninety-four unattached men would not have respected the Kunzendorf marriages or tolerated their snorting consummation in neighboring bunks if these six women had been the only available representatives of their sex. But a few minutes' walk away from the camp there was also the village of Kunzendorf, inhabited by old folk and children and several hundred widows.

The village was a German settlement that had paid its price for a German war. Almost all the male inhabitants between fifteen and fifty-five had disappeared from the village streets in the space of a few years. They left behind them land to be farmed, craft businesses to be manned, orphans to be fathered, and widows to be consoled — in short, a worldly estate in need of good husbandry. It cannot have been an accident that a camp for several hundred men with time on their hands while waiting for repatriation was sited adjacent to such a need. An impoverished state, in any case reluctant to sponsor a fund for the widows of the enemy, turned coupler instead, placed the horse before the cart and relied on natural attraction to draw them together gratis. Why should a man wait for repatriation to bring him into uncertain possession of a life he had almost forgotten, with such a palpable alternative swelling before his very eyes? Why not the taut pumpkins ripening in the gardens here, the baked apples bursting from the corsets of their skin, the round waists and full bosoms and mellow apple wine that the housewife served her famished guest on Sunday afternoons?

Why not indeed?

The colonel dubbed the artful widows the sirens of Kunzendorf, and tied himself firmly to Tschubla's mast. As for myself, I was hard of hearing. But I still had one good ear.

This good ear of mine was leavened by the invitations of a pastry maker named Henrietta Nausch. It was particularly sensitive to Henrietta's case, not only on account of the baked meats, flans and pies that came sizzling out of her oven, but because she was the widow of Hermann Nausch, the foreman of my tileworks in Deutsch-Proben, whose unfortunate fate had indirectly been my responsibility.

During the war I had received a delivery of two hundred and fifty bicycles. At the time I was worried about the possibility of air raids on Pressburg and wanted to keep warehouse inventories to a minimum. It seemed safer to put the bicycles in storage in the country, and thus I decided to evacuate them to the factory in Deutsch-Proben. There they remained untouched until the uprising in August 1944, when the partisans captured the factory and with it the two hundred and fifty bicycles. The partisans couldn't do much with a tileworks but had plenty of use for the bicycles, or would have had, if the bicycles had been equipped not only with wheels but also with tires. Where were the five hundred tires? There weren't any tires, for I had decided to import them from a separate manufacturer in Budapest, as and when they were required. Nausch had not been informed of the Hungarian whereabouts of the tires, and even if he had, the partisans would not have believed him. My prudence cost Nausch his life. The partisans shot him on the spot.

Henrietta moved west, but she moved too late. Sealed off in Mährisch-Ostrau, she sought refuge in the German colony in Kunzendorf, where she turned the flour on her widowed hands to professional account. The yeasty doughs that had fattened Hermann until the incident of the bicycle tires rose into the crust of a fragile livelihood for herself and her two young daughters. A daughterless father myself, I was disarmed by the mischievous red-headed sprites who danced in and out with crisp faces and gingerbread curls, childish samples from the same confectionery, advertising the flavor, were that necessary, of their mother's more sumptuous charms.

"Will you have a slice of the rhubarb crumble, Mr. Pallehner? Or the cheesecake, perhaps?"

Henrietta was the daughter of a Viennese pastry cook. She had been raised in the business and she had made it her own. When she leaned into the oven to juggle with her bouncing pies she demonstrated sturdy, whole-meal thighs and calves tapering from knee to ankle like rounded loaves. The flour and condiments of her father's trade must have dusted off in the marriage bed and somehow strayed into the pigment of her skin, freckling her white arms with caraway seed and saffron. And Henrietta's progenitor, oh master pieman, had lavished all his care on the dainty finishings, from the almond eyes and the delicious morsels of ears to that insolent raisin, one solitary marooned wart, blushing darkly out of the whiteness of her throat.

"Joseph, do help yourself to the strawberry flan."

Summer had come, broad-girthed and loading Henrietta's table with the cakes of the season. How should I have resisted those innocent strawberry flans, or the more potent insinuations of her custards? The conscience that might otherwise have been my ally coaxed me back to the widow's kitchen on account of Hermann, whose mortal soul had gone missing with five hundred bicycle tires. Henrietta enjoyed my company, and my appetite enlivened her art. Besides, there was the debt of my own gratitude — not merely for her catering. I had made my own contribution to that. Nightly plundering of the quartermaster's stores had lined Henrietta's shelves as well as my own stomach. No, it was more than that. Out of a scarecrow she had made a man. She found me worthy of her food. She put marrow back in the bones of my self-confidence. Already appreciative of the widow's table, I had begun to appreciate the widow's bed. Standing in the kitchen I could feel the heat of Henrietta's oven and already, in my imagination, was rising like one of her impatient pastries to the starched sheets and down coverlets in the snug little room upstairs. The executor of Hermann's will, and its self-styled beneficiary as well? It was out of the question. If I paddled in Henrietta I would drown.

I addressed my problem to the ceiling.

"Think of your family, Joseph. You have a wife and four sons. You can't let go now. After all these years . . ."

Willy's pungent advice wafted up out of the dark and made me shudder. Then what should I do? I couldn't break off my visits now.

Willy spoke.

"What you need is a chaperone."

And as it turned out, I acquired not one chaperone, but two. In the midsummer heat of the Henrietta crisis Silversdorf arrived at Kunzendorf.

On the feast day of the Assumption of the Blessed Virgin, Willy Hartmann, Silversdorf and I were invited by Henrietta's neighbor to share a brace of fatted geese. It was a quarter of an hour by train to the hamlet where Henrietta lived. I kidnapped a sack of potatoes, Willy abducted three cans of red cabbage, and Silversdorf held our hostess to ransom with wicked jokes that gave her stitches in both sides. Threatened with more she begged for mercy, and the geese were duly released from the oven. A table had been laid in the goose widow's garden. It was a cloudless summer day. The caterers demurely said grace, blessing the Virgin in whose name, and the three trenchermen sat down, unleashing ferocious appetites.

The sun burned down from its superfluous zenith on the brown-bellied, crackling geese, the first afternoon shadow picked its way through the bare ruins of their bones, but the company's attention was still divided between Henrietta's raspberries and the goose widow's conserved peaches. The trenchermen took a turn around the garden while the ladies cleared the luncheon wreckage, and already it was time for tea. No quarter was given to a cream cake that ventured foolishly onto the table, the braided pastry of an *apfelstrudel* was summarily unraveled. Three appetites choked on the granite opposition of a slab of shortbread, but were revived by an evening jug of apple wine for a brisk skirmish with assorted cold meats. Who had eyes for the sun, dipping toward the horizon? A balmy evening, the warm aftermath of day released from the terrace paving, sustained the swallow flight of Silversdorf's pleasantries through the gradually fading light and swam darkly under the table, where I was distracted by the more knobbly attentions of Henrietta's knee. Where would the goose widow's chase have led, if the remaining wind in Willy Hartmann's stomach had not suddenly erupted into an anguished shout of "By God! It's seven o'clock!" that restored us all to our senses. For by God it was, and the train for Kunzendorf left at twenty minutes past. A brisk ten-minute walk to the station — but who was brisk? Who could even walk? Willy and I could at least try, placing one foot determinedly in front of the other; but for Silversdorf, who had had no schooling in Henrietta's pies and whose shrunken innards were still attuned to prison fare, it was quite out of the question. The two widows sprang between the shafts of an antique dogcart and set out with scattering heels, conveying Silversdorf in bloated recumbency helter-skelter to the station, with Willy and myself in cold pursuit, bowlegged, hands cupped under monstrous bellies like waiters carrying stacks of plates. Only two minutes to spare there, and another nasty moment when Silversdorf became finally incapacitated a hundred yards from the gates of Kunzendorf. We had no option but to drag our fallen comrade to get him inside the camp's eight o'clock immunity literally by the skin of his heels.

In the wake of these events on the feast day of the Assumption of the Blessed Virgin, Willy and I erected a bulwark against the widow peril by forming a Club of Faithful Husbands. Ironically, our club happened to share the same initials as Tschubla's colonel, who as the camp's senior resident would have made a respected chairman but for his prior commitments, not merely elsewhere, but unequivocally in the opposite direction. Although he felt unqualified to lend us his moral support, Carl-Friedrich welcomed our initiative, animadverting only mildly that the word *league* seemed to him more suggestive of solidarity than *club*. In deference to the colonel's initial sensibilities our club was renamed accordingly.

Inevitably there were those who scoffed at LFH as the embodiment of Lofty but Futile Hopes, and many other variations were offered on the same theme. These critics had not bothered to read the statutes of our league. It was not a moral tribunal. Attachments were not excluded from membership, nor were bachelors. Our only object was to get men safely back home. The league's rules permitted widows' visits to the camp, but its members had to pledge not to set foot in widows' houses or to tend pumpkins in their gardens. For many men even this modest requirement presented too great an obstacle. They yearned, understandably, for the tranquil domesticity enshrined in their widow's own four walls; and envisaging the struggle to build a new existence back in their own country, how natural it was for them to prefer an already established niche, apparently commodious and demanding no more than physical entry to satisfy the title of ownership. To those whose inclinations or self-discipline moored them safely inside the gates of Kunzendorf it was a laughing matter, perhaps; there was no shortage of bawdy jokes that widowed the subject of its underlying seriousness. But how serious it could become when inclination and discipline drifted the other way, out of our little harbor, was made sadly evident by the case of Silversdorf.

One of the founding members of the League of Faithful Husbands, Hans Silversdorf was the first to betray it. In the weeks following the Assumption of the Blessed Virgin he was frequently absent from the camp at weekends — he went out fishing, he said, but secretly he was paying visits to the goose widow's home. One Sunday night he failed to return to the camp before curfew and on the following day, suspecting the worst, Willy and I took the train out to the hamlet where Henrietta and the goose widow lived.

We found Silversdorf reclining on the sofa in the widow's parlor, fast asleep, with a napkin still tucked into his collar on which we could identify fresh traces of liver sausage and chocolate mousse. The noise of our entrance must have woken him. He opened his eyes, took in the two bailiffs standing over him with stern faces like badges of office, and anticipating their errand said simply "I'm just very tired," closed his eyes again, and turned his face to the wall. He managed to put so much finality into this last word that I knew our mission was hopeless even before we had spoken. The chairman and secretary of the League of Faithful Husbands turned around and disconsolately caught the train back.

Stuck fast to the widow who held the golden goose, Hans Silversdorf carelessly forfeited his expatriate prisoner's immunity and enjoyed a leisurely civilian life in the rural surroundings of Kunzendorf. For the first few months he did no work, entirely preoccupied with his victuals, sleep, and the teeming duties of husbandry in the widow's fallow bed. His wife, as she soon became by a law that was either uninformed or chose to brush aside the trifling matter of Silversdorf's bigamy, worked as a secretary at the foundry where Willy had singed his boots, leaving her husband to illuminate his days with schemes for an electric mousetrap and the superfluous floodlighting of pumpkins. Silversdorf relished his freedom as the privilege of uselessness. He seemed happy enough, pottering about the house in his predecessor's slippers, pliers ready to hand. Willy and I were frequent guests. We watched him grow plump and complacent.

"You fools," he would say, as we watched his wife set on the table the dish that had given the widow her name, "look what a life I lead! It's yours for the asking. League of Faithful Husbands! Who ever heard such nonsense!" And with an air of condescension he sprinkled parsley over a steaming bowl of new potatoes.

By the time that parsley went out of season his wife's patience had also begun to wither, and in the course of our now less frequent visits it gradually transpired that the golden goose was in fact a tarnished imitation. After the wretched years of prison life the marvelous novelty of warm feet, a full belly, and a sound sleep had gravitated once again to the level of the commonplace; there were signs that Silversdorf was beginning to feel bored. He was not the man to hoe gardens with a whistle on his lips, to press apples, retile roofs, or make himself useful about the house as his wife would have desired. But what else did the Inhuman Weapon have to offer? The electric mousetrap he had been hoping to have patented turned out to be a failure, and despite the hours he spent reclining meditatively on the sofa, which his wife had once treated with tiptoeing respect, he hadn't a single bright idea to show for it. Even the midnight pumpkins remained unilluminated. What use was this capital intellect, in which the housewife invested geese and dumplings and quarts of buttermilk, if it could pay out no other dividends than dirty washing and an after-dinner snore?

Newly married and newly disappointed, Silversdorf's widow-wife turned sour. She made us unwelcome in her house. More mouths to feed, no better than her husband, loafers under the pretense of imprisonment. She lashed us with her tongue. To imagine that this harpy had once drawn her husband in a dogcart! At least we had the excuse of curfew. Silversdorf had no such immunity; only the bitter irony of the doghouse.

He got a job as an electrician with a firm in Mährisch-Ostrau. Relations with his wife improved as a result, but that honeymoon between captivity and adjustment to the realities of freedom had not been a happy experience. I learned my lesson from Silversdorf. In prison we had been suspended from the drift of history, but none of us would be able to return to the point from which he had set out. Nine years on, the outside world had almost forgotten the war. It was impatient of the dawdlers, the relics who walked numbly out of a better-forgotten past. There would be no credit for those years that had been irrecoverably lost. We had got out of step with time, and we were going to have to run very fast if we wanted to catch up.

A dogcart and two more or less able-bodied men had already rescued one chance of survival for Hans Silversdorf. He missed the next. He sank into the obscurity of a provincial town on the wrong side of the border. A multination state of the kind in which I had spent most of my life might have been able to accommodate an eccentric German, even if he were tired and aging like Silversdorf, but with the war and the subsequent changes in the political geography of Europe its human geography had changed too.

After a couple of years Silversdorf found his position increasingly difficult, and he applied to the Czechoslovakian government for resettlement in his native country. The application was not granted until five years later. He arrived back in Germany in 1960, where he died within a few months, a destitute alcoholic, a burnt-out case.

In the Poplar Avenue

D URING the six years between my departure from Dachau and my arrival in Kunzendorf I had not read a newspaper. A stray sheet, months or even years old, would sometimes emerge from a packing case, and perhaps one might be lucky enough to find a more recent fragment somewhere on the floor. No matter that the news was out-of-date and had been censored in any case — it opened a window for the prisoner to catch a glimpse of the world he had been forbidden. What greedy attention, what speculation those scraps of newsprint aroused! Passed surreptitiously from hand to hand, they fueled debates and even gave us hope, a reassurance that reality of another kind continued uninterrupted elsewhere. In Kunzendorf these marvels lay openly on the tables, fresh and in their entirety, to be rifled with impunity. We read them column for column from start to finish and back again, relishing a faded sense of dignity that the privilege of information helped to restore. But not only that, of course. The inmates of Kunzendorf were not common readers. Personal interest in the prospects of our release made us seismographers of the political drift, beneath the surface, on which we had been told those prospects depended.

The signs were not encouraging. They posted us back to

where we had come from: containment within the borders of the Soviet zone. It was all very well for Radio Free Europe to broadcast incitements to sabotage. Nine years after the war the Americans had still not come, and the saboteurs among the local population who had taken them at their word were sitting in prison for their pains. We could not trust their news either. Claims and counterclaims. We looked for a balance between the contradictions. And so the months dragged on. By the autumn of 1953 we had still not heard a word, not even the morsel of a rumor, to sustain our flagging hopes of release.

In November we decided to take action. On the initiative of the colonel, an engineer by the name of Otto Schams, Willy Hartmann, and myself, a committee was formed for the release and repatriation of the prisoners of Kunzendorf. Our number had crept up to two hundred and nine in the course of the summer and there it stayed, although there would be many more to come long after the camp had been closed down. The last arrivals, released reluctantly from the spider's web of Czechoslovakia's prisons, were all long-term prisoners who had been sentenced to at least ten years. Some of them had almost served the full time; men tired and broken, like Silversdorf, in some cases justly punished, but without contrition or even regret for crimes that they had committed long ago and could not clearly remember. They considered themselves scapegoats, plucked arbitrarily out of an army of accessories no better than themselves; resentful first and foremost of the capricious selection of fate, they overlooked the origins from which fate had made its selection, forgot that there was once a time when they had been selectors of a kind themselves.

A spokesman for the committee was elected by the inmates of the camp. One group supported the nomination of the chairman of the League of Faithful Husbands, another group put forward a rival candidate, a Communist of the old guard by the name of Koblicek. A Communist of whatever persuasion, even one who had been imprisoned like Koblicek, could not have carried a vote on anything in Kunzendorf, and I was elected by a large majority.

The Koblicek group was represented on our committee, however, and did its best to torpedo our deliberations from the start. We proposed a hunger strike as the most effective way of drawing the attention of Prague to our case. Koblicek was against the proposal. A meeting of all the camp inmates was convened in the main barrack, where the motion was put to the assembly and again carried by an overwhelming majority. Koblicek's group failed to put forward a convincing argument against the hunger strike, for reasons that were perfectly clear to the rest of us: they were in cahoots with the camp staff and did not wish to be associated with an action that would be an embarrassment to the government in Prague. Some of them may just have been opportunists, but others had been planted as stooges who would be carried by the tide of homecoming prisoners onto the other side of the border, where they would conveniently be issued with identity cards by the government against whom it would be their business to spy.

The terms of the hunger strikers' vote, unanimous but for a dozen names that were probably already familiar to a certain ministry in Prague, were laid out in a long telegram that we dispatched ourselves from the village post office: as of the date of dispatch the inmates of the camp at Kunzendorf would go on a hunger strike until they had received official confirmation from the authorities in Prague of the date of their release and safe-conduct home.

In the interests of solidarity we agreed that no visits outside the camp would be allowed while the hunger strike lasted, and to conserve our strength nobody would work either. An eerie stillness settled over the compound. Prisoners strolled out in groups, lounged and talked, played cards or simply lay on their bunks. Three days passed. Nothing happened. We nursed the emptiness in our bellies and remained firm in our resolution. The camp staff scoffed and watched us with hostility. The fifth or sixth day would be the turning point. The solidarity of empty stomachs could not be stretched beyond a week, and once a few had succumbed the cause was lost. What if Prague decided to wait it out? What if they didn't come?

They came with the first snowfall, at the beginning of December. On the fifth morning of the hunger strike two black limousines drove through the camp gates and pulled up outside the office of the *Lagerkommandant*. The occupants of the car, five in all, filed into the office and remained closeted there for half an hour. A delegation of the hunger strikers, including myself and the colonel, waited outside in the snow. At last the door opened and the *Kommandant* himself emerged. He asked if the colonel and I were authorized to speak in the strikers' name. We said we were. He told us to come in.

In the presence of the envoys from Prague, including two silent men whom the colonel identified by their uniforms as officers of the NKGB, we repeated our demands and the guarantees we would require if the hunger strike were to be broken off. One of the envoys explained that bulk transport was logistically not possible, but that as of Christmas the prisoners would be released each week in batches of ten, so that by late spring all the inmates of the camp would have been sent home. The envoy said he had been authorized to make this offer by the government in Prague. Was the arrangement acceptable to us? I said it was, but that we would want confirmation from the other side before breaking off our strike. I suggested sending a cable to my wife, outlining the proposal we had just heard, with instructions to get in touch with Theodor Oberländer, the responsible minister in the government of the country that now bore the for us unfamiliar name of the Federal Republic of Germany, and to ask him to obtain confirmation through official channels, which my wife would relay back to me. The delegation agreed to my suggestion, and the cable to my wife was sent off immediately.

On the afternoon of the sixth day I received a cable from my wife, confirming the proposal made to us by the delegation from Prague. We called off the strike and celebrated our victory.

During the couple of weeks between the end of the strike and Christmas intense excitement buzzed through the camp. Some of the inmates packed their belongings, like impatient schoolboys, as soon as the news was announced, and carried their bags around wherever they went. There were others, by contrast, who seemed to have slowed down and become thoughtful at the news of their impending release. The attachments were among this group. Tschubla's nocturnal visits to the colonel ceased; the two of them began taking long walks out into the country instead. Their problems were obvious enough. But beside those tangled feelings of relief, excitement, and incredulousness that each of us had, more of one and less of the other, according to individual temperament, we all had our secret misgivings about what awaited us on the other side of the border.

To make us at least outwardly presentable to the critical eyes that would be watching us when we were deposited on the doorstep of capitalism at Schirnding station the administration of Kunzendorf had fed its charges very well. We were its present to the West, Christmas geese that had been fattened out of season so that when our time came we could be exported in plump and palatable condition.

Not one of us could have resisted being fed in order to vindicate a lean principle, but when, on top of that, it came to being dressed up and packaged in a new suit of clothes supplied gratis by an open-handed socialist government, the Kunzendorf geese raised a cackle of protest.

A notice to the effect that all prisoners were to apply to the quartermaster to be fitted free of charge for a new suit was debated by a vociferous assembly in the main barrack. The colonel called on us to support a boycott of this scandalous offer: it was a cheap bribe, a whitewash, and anyone who accepted it compromised his integrity. What integrity was there left to compromise, countered his adversary sneeringly, a thin and battered general who had only recently been released from arctic Soviet captivity in the prisoner-of-war camp at Archangelsk. Hang it all, we were prisoners, weren't we, defeated in a war that was a permanent disgrace to our country. Which of us felt qualified to speak of his integrity? The general challenged the assembly in a cracked, tremulous voice. He waited for a full minute. Nobody spoke up. Well then, resumed the general, at least we could attempt a formal show of dignity; he for his part intended to spare his wife the ordeal of greeting a ragamuffin, the ruins of the man she remembered from ten years previously. He would take advantage of the offer, damn it. He would wear a socialist suit home.

Only a small number of prisoners took the general's view. I sided with the colonel. For me it was quite unthinkable that I should wear propaganda on my back on behalf of a country that had imprisoned me for seven years. The arguments between the two sides were bitter. How easily the solidarity that had flourished during the hunger strike withered in the December frost! On account of a suit of clothes!

For a few days the rancor lingered on, but it was soon overlaid by a more serious concern that was shared by us all. The weeks had limped forward, it was almost Christmas, but apart from some rapid tailoring by the seamstresses in Kunzendorf there was no evidence at all that arrangements were being made for our departure. On December the twenty-third a weary delegation paid a second visit to the *Lagerkommandant* to present another ultimatum. Unless steps were taken immediately to arrange for our transport back home we would go on a hunger strike again. The *Kommandant* put a call through to a ministry in Prague and handed me the telephone. A voice at the other end of the line apologized for the delay that had been caused by the unusually heavy demands of the Christmas traffic and assured me that transports would still proceed as planned before the end of the year. I asked for a specific date. The voice hesitated and disappeared for a few minutes, emerging from a muffled conference to announce that transports would begin on December the twenty-ninth.

Not Christmas geese, then, but New Year fare. Not knowing what names would be called out for the first transport, we all began to make our preparations. Willy and I, waiving the league's rules on this one last occasion, walked out on Christmas day to take our leave of Silversdorf and Henrietta Nausch. Henrietta baked a magnificent farewell cake, loaded with all the seductions of her art, which we ate in festive gloom. It was the seventh Christmas I had spent in captivity, and in some ways it was the saddest.

Early on the morning of the twenty-ninth two hundred and three men and six women assembled for *Appell* in the compound. One of the black limousines that had brought the Prague delegation to Kunzendorf at the beginning of the month stood parked inside the gates. Two Czech civilians and an NKGB officer in uniform had been quartered in the village to supervise the transports during the following weeks. A list of a dozen names was read out by the

Lagerkommandant. Koblicek was among them. The tendency of the list could be identified by the conspicuous number of suitwearers it included. There they went, the rats! Scuttling for their holes before the rest of us arrived to put forward any compromising evidence. The men muttered and trudged back to their barracks. None of us had expected to be among the first to go. But we had all hoped.

I took advantage of the presence of the NKGB officer, who stood waiting by the gates while the transportees were collecting their bags, to broach a matter that had been weighing on my mind. I asked him if it were true that a conference of the four powers would be taking place in Berlin at the beginning of the year.

He shrugged.

"What about it? Is that of any concern to you?"

He spoke Czech without the slightest accent.

"Well," I said, "maybe it is. At the rate these transports are being arranged, some of us won't be home until May. I've read that the reunification of Germany is one of the points on the agenda of the Berlin Conference. What if it fails to reach an agreement? Your government is quite capable of taking retaliatory measures. And for all I know that might include suspending the repatriation of German prisoners."

The man laughed and flashed his teeth.

"Of course the Berlin Conference will fail to reach an agreement. But that's not going to have the slightest effect on any of you."

"Then why don't you arrange for transports in bigger lots? Why not twenty men at a time? Or fifty? And why don't you let us have the list in advance, so that each of us knows when to expect his turn?"

"There are technical problems," he replied curtly, and turned away.

How tired I was of these self-important, secretive men! How I hated these endless evasions and secrets!

A week later we went through the same rigmarole. Two hundred tense men on parade, a dozen men called out, with two nurses thrown in for good measure. We were the tail-enders, but the bureaucrats in Prague still contrived to put quite a sting in the tail. Not one of the members of the committee that had organized the hunger strike to agitate for our earlier release had been included in the first two lists. The pattern was depressingly clear: good boys and fence sitters would be given priority. And so it went on, week for week. The transport lots reached a peak of sixteen at the end of January and dropped to nine at the beginning of February. The following week there was no transport at all. Panic broke out. Siberian rumors inevitably began to do the rounds. The prisoners mobbed the office of the *Kommandant* and demanded to know what was going on. "Technical problems," they were told. Days dragged by in dreadful suspense. The political situation was sensitive. In the newspapers we read commentaries, for me with chilling echoes of the voice of Tibor Benjamin Lazar and its evocation of the great wheel, on the forthcoming trial in Bratislava of Husak and Novomesky and their fellow "bourgeois nationalists." But a week later the transports were resumed: grace for a further eleven men. What a cruel waiting! Among the ringleaders of the hunger strike there was growing unease. Eight transports already gone, and not one of us had been included. What if the Czechs backtracked? Who would miss a dozen men who had been gone since the end of the war if they failed to reappear from an almost posthumous existence on the dark side of the border?

By the middle of February we were down to ninety-four men. To economize on fuel the camp administration closed down half the barracks and moved us into the remaining huts. No more widows came to visit us now, nobody went out to work, the quartermaster shut his store, the *Kommandant* abandoned his office for half the week and only one guard was posted at the camp gates. On February the twenty-second a big push forward: twenty names called out, among them Willy Hartmann. The eerie spell seemed to have been broken at last. I took my leave of my friend, embracing him at the camp gates. Seventy-four men shared the accommodation of a dozen huts with a silence enlivened by little more than their memories. The colonel went at the beginning of March. Fifty-six left. Fuel was running out and we were told there would be no more deliveries. We crouched in the barracks and watched the snow drift like a shroud across the deserted compound. Kunzendorf had become a ghost town.

To escape the camp's depressing atmosphere Otto Schams and I took long walks down the poplar avenue by the river. It was a very long avenue. It seemed to have no end. For us it ended when the daylight faded and forced us to turn back. How quickly the darkness encroached behind us and swallowed up our steps! How quickly it snatched the past from our heels as we trudged homewards down the poplar avenue! Somewhere along that endless white avenue Otto had said "We'd better head for home," and already the future we had been facing had become a past on which we turned our backs, snatched from under our heels and lost in utter darkness. We peered forward into the night. A faint sheen of snow marked the road ahead, and Otto prodded his question at me like a blind man groping with a stick.

"What'll you do when you get home?"

"I shall start up a toy factory," I said without a moment's hesitation.

My reply astonished myself. It was an idea that had never occurred to me before.

"There's no harm in that," remarked Otto, and of course that was exactly what I meant.

This conversation in the poplar avenue took place on March the fifth.

Three days later the fifty-six remaining men assembled in the compound to hear the weekly transport list announced. Sixteen names were on the list. Mine was the last.

When he had finished reading out the list the *Kommandant* said that two further transports were planned. The last forty detainees would be evacuated from Kunzendorf by the beginning of April.

Ten minutes for the sixteen men on this week's transport to get their baggage and fall in outside the camp gates! Suddenly a hurry to get on, an interval measured in minutes, as if we had not spent aching years waiting for this moment. And so it was a hurried ceremony of farewell that took place at the gates of Kunzendorf. A line of shabby men set out along a white deserted road with bags and bundles tied up with string. Only now was the war over for us.

The spectacle of two Pullman cars, inscribed with the gold lettering of a faded splendor, awaited us at the dingy village station. We might decline to wear their suits, but at least we would travel back in style. Furnishings in gilt and mahogany, plush upholstery, stucco cornices and coats of arms: a saloon of luxurious elegance. We felt like intruders, hesitating to put our grimy bundles on the carpeted floors. Oppressed by the magnificence into which we had been betrayed, we traveled the twenty miles to Mährisch-Ostrau in silence.

At Ostrava there was a halt of half an hour. The Kunzendorf escort clambered reluctantly out of the Pullman and returned to the obscurity of their village. They were replaced by four security officers, three men and a woman, in sleek uniforms and highly polished boots. I sat alone in the compartment of the saloon next to the door and listened to the four officers conferring in undertones in the passageway. One of them came in and walked up and down the car with a bundle of files, calling out the name on the cover of the file and switching it to the bottom of the pile as each man answered. All present and more or less correct. The officer pulled open a window and stretched out an arm. I heard a whistle blow. The car gave a slight jerk and rolled forward. Destination: Prague.

Two of the security officers disappeared into the other car. I turned to the window and looked out. I must have slipped into a reverie, for I did not notice when the woman officer sat down opposite me. Turning away from the window, I saw her watching me with an expressionless face.

"I hope you have no objection to my company," she said without even the trace of a smile as I caught her eye.

"Not at all . . ."

She must have been in her early forties, about ten years younger than myself. She had a handsome face, hardened by some austerity other than the rather angular jaw and high Slav cheekbones. She returned my gaze with composure, blowing elegant smoke rings toward the ceiling, and said, "Would you care for a cigarette?"

"Thank you, I've given it up. I once knew a man called Thonet —"

I didn't finish the sentence. My eye was caught by a couple of files lying on the seat beside her. Presumably one of them was mine, and presumably this woman had read it. What was she doing here? Why did she want to talk to me? A sudden instinct of caution held me back.

"Thonet?" queried the woman, waiting for me to go on.

"Thonet had a problem with smoking, you see."

I was wide awake now, sitting on the edge of the seat, my mind racing. Memories of Esterhazy, the road builder, and half a dozen others I had known who had been turned back at the border. We aren't out of Czechoslovakia yet, I thought. They coddle us with the illusion of safety in the improbable luxury of this Pullman car, put a woman agent into the car, an attractive woman who offers cigarettes and asks sympathetic questions. Plenty of time. A long way to Prague, and as long again to the border. Plenty of time to listen to foolish men blab, perhaps pick up a new charge on the way, open dossiers on blabbing men and put them on trial and — who could say? Recycle them perhaps. Feed them back into the system for another seven years. Leopoldov. The fortress dungeons. My God! I felt my hands begin to sweat.

Somewhere along the line the train pulled to a halt, perhaps for a signal. The woman got up and walked down the car. I heard her exchange remarks with her colleague at the other end.

But after a minute she came back and sat down again. I wondered what she had been talking to the other security officer about. Outside it was beginning to grow dark. The train waited. She started to ask me more questions. I felt increasingly uneasy. Perhaps the train was waiting for my answers. What did I think about Communism? I said I didn't think anything about Communism. I said I had spent seven years thinking about nothing other than how to get through my term of imprisonment alive. Seven years? The woman feigned surprise. What had I done to be given as long a sentence as that? I told her she would find all the details she wanted to know in the folder that was lying on the seat beside her. Only then must she have grasped what was at the back of my mind. She laughed. Don't worry, she said, we're as anxious to be rid of you as you are of us. She took out a newspaper. And as if this were the sign it had been waiting for, the train suddenly began to move.

We spent the rest of the journey to Prague in silence. It was already night when we arrived. The woman folded her newspaper and got up. She and the three other security officers disappeared for almost an hour. I noticed they locked the door between the saloon and the corridor. Hardly to keep us in. More likely to keep unwanted passengers out.

The train stood. Why this waiting again?

At last they came back. They had arranged for coffee and sandwiches to be brought to the car. A final fattening of the geese. Coffee and sandwiches. No, we had wanted for nothing. The train lurched out of the discreet siding where it had waited for an hour and a half and left the lights of the city behind. I pushed the half-eaten sandwiches aside. My throat was so dry I could not swallow.

I watched the moon rise beyond gold reflections of the carriage lamps and the woman's shadowy face. Traces of snow lit up like phosphorous flares in the surrounding dark. Prague lay behind us, the train carried its warm enclosures of light and ran quickly through the night toward the border in the West. A long, long, long journey, travel and travail, the journey on which I had labored all these long years. A wife whom I had not, a son whom I had never, seen since the day I set out. How had she changed? And how had he become? Less hours now to wait than years already waited, but the years seemed to have become hours and the hours years. Would I find acceptance, in my borrowed coat and boots tied together with string? Would they even recognize me? Privileged to be myself, would I recognize myself? I began to tremble so violently that the coffee jumped out of my cup and spilled onto the table.

The woman pushed a napkin over toward me and asked quietly, "Excited?"

"Excited!" I blurted out angrily. "Do you know what it means to have been taken away from your family for years? From your husband? From an unborn child you have never seen?"

She looked away and said nothing. I leaned back into the seat, put my hands under the table and gripped them between my knees. Excited! What word could have expressed the standing torrent of sensations that vaulted back out of the memory of my soul, the anguish and desolation, bitterness, hope and love that I experienced in one moment! I was the groaning river come alive at the end of winter fastness, I was the spume breaking over the sand on the far side of the ocean. I had made the crossing, I was alive, my heart ablaze inside me. Excited? I felt as if the bones were melting in my body, liquid tallow poised in one swelling, momentous drop about to fall. The moon swam clear of the clouds and brightened the sky. Moon! The bright night sky! In the wake of the naked ascendant moon the carriage lamps dimmed the reflected lights they hung out in the sky, and the face of the woman underneath seemed to drift just a little out of focus. Her face was moving. Tears were rolling down her cheeks. Tears? Yes, tears. And from the face in the window another voice softly began to speak.

"Yes, I know what it means to have lost these things. It was in . . . ah, but what does the year matter? It was early in the war. My husband and I belonged to a resistance group. Someone betrayed the group. We were arrested, my husband was shot and I was sent to Dachau. I had a three-month-old baby at the time. A boy. A son. And I didn't see him again for five years. I came home after the war and looked for the features of the baby I remembered in the face of a five-year-old boy. The same and not the same. How that baby had grown! I saw in him his father. I had come home to meet my son, not expecting I would also meet a living memory of my husband. He was alive in the boy. And so the meeting with my own child turned out to be a very painful joy. . . . Yes, I know what it means to have been taken from my family. I wanted to tell you that. My prison was your home, my home has been your prison, but does that difference matter now? There is more, so much more, you see, that we have in common. My train went the other way, but I sat in it with the same feelings that you have now. . . ."

I was stunned by what she told me. Who was this other woman who had talked to me out of the window? I turned and saw her. Yes, there she sat. How she had changed in these few minutes! The mask had dropped from her face. How gentle it had become! And I had thought — what had I thought? I could no longer remember, no longer cared. I reached across the table and pressed her hand. I would have spoken if I could, but my voice choked in my throat.

The train began to slow down. We sat in silence, our faces turned again toward the window. The moon had climbed up out of sight. Passing clouds, light and shadow, the landscape briefly seen then indistinct, rising and falling back into the darkness.

"Look!"

The sign of the eagle, emblem of another country, another sovereignty, loomed up and was already past.

Seven years.

The train crossed the border a few minutes after midnight.